WESTMAR CO

P9-CQE-424

BEN D. WOOD

EDUCATIONAL REFORMER

By
Matthew T. Downey

LB
885
.W65
D6

92
W873d

Library of Congress Catalog Number 65–23014
Copyright 1965 by Educational Testing Service. All rights reserved.
Princeton, New Jersey

58150

Table of Contents

Acknowledgments

When the author agreed to write this biographical sketch of Ben D. Wood, he had encountered the man's name perhaps a dozen times in books. During the following months a large number of people came to his aid to help him fill in the career which the name represented. He is indebted especially to Frank Bowles, Henry Chauncey, John A. Downing, Hart Fessenden, John C. Flanagan, Reynold B. Johnson, Dwayne Orton, Sir James Pitman, Donald J. Shank, Eugene R. Smith, George D. Stoddard, Herbert A. Toops, Arthur E. Traxler, Grace Turner, and Thomas J. Watson, Jr. These persons also helped to place Wood's career in the historical perspective of the testing and guidance movement and saved the author from several errors of omission and interpretation.

The author incurred his greatest single debt to Ben D. Wood. Conversations that lasted through several pleasant summer afternoons gave him the beginning of an appreciation for the personality behind the name and the career. For anyone familiar with Wood's scholarly orientation and respect for independent thought, it is unnecessary to add that he respected the author's complete freedom to use and to interpret information about him whatever its source.

To the staff of the Educational Testing Service the author is grateful for numerous acts of assistance rendered in a characteristically competent and friendly manner.

M.T.D.

FABIAN BACHRACH

Dr. Benjamin DeKalbe Wood posed for this picture in January 1965.

An Introduction

O WRITE the life of a living man involves a risk. It is too easy to get involved: to write for his causes rather than about them. Although the risk was especially grave in the case of Ben D. Wood, it has been taken. In a monumental and perhaps not always successful effort to maintain critical detachment, the author did gain an appreciation for the personality of his subject. He felt the tremendous pull of a remarkable human being. Biographers of the dead miss this. Yet to miss this would have been to miss the essence of Ben Wood.

Ben Wood is one of the most extraordinary individuals this writer has encountered. His ability to inspire others to think boldly, to teach intelligently, or to act sanely, is one of his professional trademarks. This also greatly complicates the problem of assessing his career. Wood has had an indirect influence through the innumerable people whose thoughts or whose lives he has shaped or changed.

The most impressive facet of this remarkable man is his intellectual vitality. At the age of 70 he still has most of the intellectual vigor of his youth. He thinks, relates, ponders and speculates incessantly. Whatever he has lost in mental agility with the passing of time, and it cannot be very much, he has compensated for by a tendency to think more about the moral and philosophical implications of things and ideas. Like all reformers, Wood is an optimist. He believes the world can be changed by good men promoting right ideas. He is a thinker who acts—a man involved in the world. Wood's conviction that men can change the world is an inspiring and contagious thing. It has moved innumerable people to act. One of his long-time associates, Arthur E. Traxler, Executive Director of the Educational Records Bureau, has ventured to rank Wood as "the most persuasive man in education today."[1] That could easily be true.

There was a time when a visit with Ben Wood must have seemed like an inspection of a battle front. The positions which he took at various times made him the target for educational conservatives and progressives alike. An afternoon with Ben Wood is still an adventure. It is the feeling of being on the leading edge of things. Wood has always kept about 30 years ahead of the current fashions in American education. A serious conversation with him about education is like a private preview of the future. Wood is a mind stretcher. He encourages prophetic, forward-looking thinking, and therein lies another part of his attraction. Mapping out the future is always exhilarating business.

Wood's future-mindedness has led him into a number of pioneering ventures in education. With the cooperation of the Eastman Kodak Company in 1927, he made the first major research study of the potential of motion pictures as teaching aids. He was also among the first to investigate the possibilities of the typewriter as a basic learning device for elementary schools. The first modern cumulative record card to be widely adopted in the United States was designed by Ben Wood. He was also largely responsible for the development of the first test scoring machine by the International Business Machines Corporation.

Wood is perhaps most widely known as one of the pioneers of the objective testing movement, with which he has been closely identified since the beginning of his professional career. His first book was a research study of the use of objective tests for measurement and guidance at the college level. At various times in his career he has aided the development of new tests, including tests of professional knowledge for teachers, lawyers, accountants, surgeons and dentists. He was the technical adviser to the Pennsylvania Study, the first state-wide evaluative testing survey. He also founded the Cooperative Test Service, which is now a division of the Educational Testing Service.

There are good reasons for associating Wood's name with the testing movement. Still, it is something like associating the Wright brothers with bicycle shops or Michelangelo with paint brushes. The new objective-type tests were Wood's tools. "I have all along not considered myself a test maker or a test peddler, but a tactical practi-

---

[1]All references and notes may be found in the *Notes* section on pages 93-100, numbered sequentially within each chapter.

tioner who, like a medical practitioner, uses precision instruments which fit his purpose," he says.[2] To view Wood as primarily a testing man is to misinterpret his career and to misjudge the man. "Ben Wood was never a one-idea man," George D. Stoddard, Distinguished Professor of Education, New York University, has said. "He has a roving mind that moves with equal sureness over the problems of education or of the military. He is a witty and incisive critic."[3] He was and still is a protagonist for a philosophy of education that requires tests for its proper implementation.

The principal task of Wood's life has been his effort to remold the educational system to make it more responsive to the needs of individuals. He has questioned the value of the administrative structure of the American educational system as well as the traditional philosophy of teaching. The graded school and fixed school curriculum, he contends, reflect administrative and teaching convenience, and curriculum fashions, rather than a sincere concern for individual students. Wood believes that the central and most stubborn problem still besetting American education is to make the educational system more responsive to the individual.

One asks if Wood is disappointed in the progress toward individualization, since much of the criticism which he directed at the educational system of the 1920's and 1930's is still valid. After a moment's hesitation, he replies that he is disappointed but that he is also more hopeful now than ever before. "The whole atmosphere is so different now than it was when I arrived on the scene 40 years ago with my lance and white horse. I got knocked down every other day then." He is hopeful because of the new educational technology, especially learning machines and electronic learning carrels, which will make individual learning easier and more efficient. Several recent administrative and methodological experiments, such as the ungraded high school and the new teaching alphabet, promise more rapid progress in the future. Although he admits that progress has been slow, Wood also acknowledges that many of his proposals have been adopted. "I still feel that I am one of the most fortunate people in education because I have actually lived to see many of the important things that I have advocated not only accepted but put into practice."[4]

In addition to a long career in education, Ben Wood has contributed time and effort to public and military affairs. He served as an Army psychologist during the First World War, with the rank of First Lieutenant, and from 1924 to 1934 was Captain in the Military Intelligence Officers Reserve Corps. He has acted as educational adviser to several state governments and to the federal government. He designed and directed the program for introducing an air-age and air-conscious curriculum in the nation's schools during the Second World War. After the war Wood helped design the curriculum for the new Air Force Academy. Since 1943 he has been a member of the Board of Curators of Stephens College. More recently Wood has played a major part in introducing Sir James Pitman's Initial Teaching Alphabet into the United States.

Ben Wood has led a very busy life. Nevertheless, he summarizes his own life's work as only a prelude. "As I view it, I have worked on what is but a puny and thin prologue for the grand opera which must be composed. It must be the work of many, quickly orchestrated by our finest talents, and put on the stage for a long run at the dynamic center of human affairs. Then education will fulfill what I believe to be its true destiny, that is, to help civilization survive and grow to ever higher levels of moral as well as material well-being."[5]

An Unorthodox Beginning

HE SCHOOL HOUSE did not play a very large part in Ben Wood's life during his early years. He was born in 1894 at Brownsville, Texas, and grew up on cattle ranches along the Rio Grande. His family pulled up its roots repeatedly as it trekked across southern Texas in search of better grass and water. With public schools few and far between in that area at the beginning of the century, Wood received only scattered bits of formal education prior to college. He spent one year attending the junior high school in a converted jail in the town of Rio Grande, Texas. He had about two years of high school study at Mission, Texas. Immediately before entering college in 1913 he spent one semester at the high school at Brownsville. All of these were nonaccredited schools, so Wood entered college officially without elementary or high school credits.[1]

A substantial part of Ben Wood's early education came from a crate of books which managed to survive all the uprootings of the family. It contained Rollin's *Ancient History,* Chambers' *Encyclopedia,* and the works of Plato, Quintilian, and other classical writers. He learned a great deal, of course, from the vigorous life around him. He developed an awareness of language and became bilingual through his contact with the predominantly Spanish-speaking population of the Texas border. The harsh and arid countryside gave him an introduction to classical economic thought. "I knew all about the Malthusian theory from practical experience. Each year ranchers had to sell for slaughter part of the herd to leave enough water and grass for the remainder." From personal experience Wood also learned that academic credits based on time served in a classroom are an incomplete measure of a child's knowledge.

"I have always been regarded as something of a maverick," Wood says. Like the minds of successful inventors, Wood's mind has always been receptive to unorthodox thoughts. His early years were an unorthodox beginning for a career in education, but they probably hold the most important key to understanding his success. "Just as the twig is bent the tree's inclined," is one of his favorite aphorisms.

Wood first came into contact with the developing science of educational psychology and its counterpart, educational measurement, at the University of Texas. He had the good fortune to take courses there from Professor Truman L. Kelley, a psychologist and statistician who was to become one of the leading men in the field. At the University, Wood also further nurtured his interest in language. He graduated in 1917 with a double major in educational psychology and Spanish-American literature and with membership in Phi Beta Kappa.

The United States was already at war in 1917 when Wood graduated from college. He promptly offered his services to Major Robert M. Yerkes, who was then mobilizing American psychologists for the war effort. Wood served first as a civilian psychologist at Camp Lee, Virginia, and later as a commissioned officer. As a First Lieutenant he was stationed mainly at Camp Cody, New Mexico, where he apparently became a sort of military jack-of-all-trades. His *vita* describes his Camp Cody period as "First Lieutenant, Division of Military Psychology, Camp Intelligence Officer and Camp Judge Advocate." During his last four months at the camp he was also in charge of a small segment of a rehabilitation center for shell shock victims.

Wood was discharged from the Army in May 1919, and went immediately to New York to join Truman L. Kelley as an assistant on a test constructing project sponsored by the National Research Council. Wood spent one sweltering summer cooped up in the attic of the Horace Mann School at Columbia, helping with the statistical work that led to the National Intelligence Test. In the fall he enrolled at Columbia University to study for advanced degrees in educational psychology and educational guidance and personnel administration.

When Wood began his graduate work at Columbia under E. L. Thorndike's direction in 1919, the testing movement was still in its early dawn. Only the year before Thorndike had stated his famous dictum: "Whatever exists at all exists in some amount." It followed logically that intelligence or the mental abilities necessary for success in college must exist in some amount. In an effort to measure the amount of intelligence of prospective freshmen, Columbia College had begun to experiment with psychological examinations for admissions purposes. Wood became interested in the Columbia admissions experiment and made it the subject of his doctoral dissertation. When it appeared as a book in 1923, under the title *Measurement in Higher Education*, Wood's dissertation became the first published research report on the use of the new-type tests at the college level. In the opinion of George D. Stoddard, "It was an excellent book that filled a great gap."[2]

To make the college testing experiment his dissertation topic was also a fortuitous choice for Wood because it brought him into contact with Herbert E. Hawkes, Dean of Columbia College. The Dean had furnished data and helpful suggestions for the study. Dean Hawkes liked Wood and appointed him his assistant in 1921. Hawkes exerted an important influence on Wood's life, and their association was doubtlessly responsible for deepening Wood's interest in students as individuals. Wood has said of him: "As a person he was, as you know, instinctively friendly, and as an educator he was dominated by the feeling that the major objective, to which all other school and college objectives should be instrumental, was the best and fullest development of the personality of each student as an individual." At many points in Wood's career, Hawkes's support and influence smoothed the way for accomplishments that might otherwise have been impossible.[3]

As assistant to Dean Hawkes, Wood was responsible for advising students who were preparing to enter the University's professional divisions of business, journalism, and law at the end of their third year. This experience made him more fully aware of the need for devices to predict a student's probable performance in various professional schools. An attempt to fill partially the need at Columbia led Wood to further research with objective tests. Wood discovered quite early in his career that effective educational guidance depended upon continuous educational research.

Dean Hawkes persuaded the University administration to create a professorship in Collegiate Educational Research in 1923 and, upon his recommendation, Wood was appointed to the position. Shortly thereafter, Wood's office became officially known as the Bureau of Collegiate Educational Research. It was one of the first testing and guidance bureaus set up by a liberal arts college. Although the bureau remained an adjunct of the Dean's office, Dean Hawkes did not intend that Wood confine himself to research projects in the college. "He constantly emphasized the essential unity and continuity of the educational process from kindergarten through university, and the consequent need for enlightened and humane dealing with pupils throughout the whole educational ladder," Wood says.[4] In the years to come, Wood's research projects and his educational interests would range from kindergarten to graduate school.

The principal concern of Wood's research bureau at the beginning was the improvement of educational measurement and guidance at Columbia. It was on Wood's advice that placement tests were first introduced in the college. In collaboration with A. A. Méras, Professor of French at Teachers College, Columbia University, and Suzanne Roth, of the Department of Foreign Languages, New York Public Schools, Wood constructed a placement test in French based on a word count of widely used textbooks and experimental evidence.[5] It was a milestone in test construction. A fellow educator accurately predicted that the objective language tests and word frequency counts would revolutionize "our entire teaching of modern foreign languages both in content and method."[6] He also undertook studies to determine the value of objective tests in fields of instruction in which the new tests had not yet been introduced, such as law and medicine. One advantage of the objective test over the essay test was its greater reliability and comparability—the scores of similar groups of students tended to be similar. It was essential for course examinations in professional schools to be reliable and consistent if course grades were to be used as a criterion of success for developing prognostic tests.

During the academic year 1922-1923 Wood investigated the examination practices in the Columbia Law School. At the insistence of Dean Harlan F. Stone, later Chief Justice of the United States Supreme Court, a skeptical law faculty invited Wood to experiment with new types of examinations. He began with an exhaustive study of law school records over a period of six years, concentrating on the grade distributions in various courses in successive years. He found that either the classes or the examinations varied considerably and he suspected it was the latter. To become better informed about the methods of instruction and the nature of law study, Wood regularly attended law school courses for a semester. He concluded that "nowhere in the educational world, except perhaps in other law schools, was there a more unmitigated dependence upon the traditional three-hour written examination." The examination policies were highly individualistic and the examinations highly subjective.[7]

In collaboration with three members of the Columbia Law School faculty, Wood prepared a battery of objective tests which were administered during the spring examination period in 1923. The test in Equity was constructed by Dean Stone himself. Wood concluded from subsequent correlation studies that "the new type measures what the old type measures, and does it with greater reliability." Dean Stone doubted that Columbia would wish to give up completely the essay and case method type examination but acknowledged that "Professor Wood has proceeded far enough with his studies to make it reasonably clear that the results of the traditional type of examination are more variable and uncertain than most of us had suspected and that the variations and uncertainties may be materially reduced by the use, to some extent at least, of a new type of examination."[8] Examinations partly made of objective questions were a regular feature of the Columbia Law School thereafter.

Upon learning of the successful results of the new-type law tests, Justice Benjamin N. Cardozo of the New York State Court of Appeals asked Dean Stone if similar tests might help correct the flagrant weaknesses of the New York State Bar Examination. Dean Stone suggested to Justice Cardozo that he should ask the Board of Bar Examiners, which operated under the jurisdiction of the Court of Appeals, to call on Ben Wood. For several years thereafter Wood worked intimately with Philip J. Wickser, a member and secretary of the New York State Board of Bar Examiners, to improve the State examinations. Together they produced six new-type law examinations in 1925-1926. Wood also assisted in the selection and training of the first objective test specialist employed by the Board. After examining several of the improved New York Bar examinations, Justice Stone wrote to Wickser: "The Bar owes to you and your associates, a debt of gratitude for the good work you are doing."[9]

During the academic year 1924-1925 Wood made several studies with objective-type tests in the Columbia College of Physicians and Surgeons. He helped the faculty to devise tests in pharmacology and anatomy, each of which indicated a higher degree of validity than the traditional essay examinations. In the spring of 1925 the Department of Orthopaedic Surgery adopted the new-type tests exclusively.[10]

To permit Wood to continue and to broaden his research to improve examinations, the Commonwealth Fund gave Columbia University a grant of $12,000 in November 1924. Under this subvention the Bureau of Collegiate Educational Research undertook a number of projects, beginning with a survey of examining practices in American and Canadian colleges. In its effort to determine the extent of the use of the new-type examinations, the Bureau collected 7,000 final examinations given by 65 colleges in the spring of 1925. The report concluded that the extent of the shift toward the new-type test indicated that a major revolution in examination policy was under way throughout the United States and Canada.[11]

Among the Commonwealth Fund projects were several of considerable importance to the State of New York. In cooperation with James Sullivan and Avery W. Skinner of the New York State Education Department, the Bureau of Collegiate Educational Research developed the first objective tests in physics, French, Spanish, and German used in the New York State Regents Examination. Wood considered this an especially important breakthrough for objective testing. "For the first time in the history of American education, we shall have a comprehensive objective survey of public instruction in four subject matters on a state-wide basis," he said in the spring of 1925.[12] The hand scoring of the Regents Examination confronted the Bureau with an enormous task. It also led Wood to a fortunate discovery: the administrative ability of his wife, Eleanor Perry Wood. The objective tests were scored at Albany by a brigade of workers organized and supervised by Mrs. Wood.

The Regents testing project of 1925 marked the beginning of a long and continuing association between Ben Wood and the New York State Education Department. Since 1942 he has served as a member of the State Examinations Board and has helped to shape the present educational philosophy and examining policies of the State Education Department. At the State Examination Board's annual meeting in December 1964, Wood was presented with a Certificate of Appreciation in recognition of his valuable service to the State of New York.

While he was undertaking the Commonwealth Fund studies, Wood also agreed to assist in the construction of new-type tests in Spanish and French for the junior high schools of New York City. With the aid of several language experts and with the active cooperation of Jacob Greenberg, director of foreign languages in the New York City junior high schools, Wood prepared sets of new-type language examinations and analyzed the results after they were administered. The experiment was repeated a year later for verification. In 1927 the Modern Foreign Language Study published the results of Wood's junior high school and Regents testing experiments under the title *New York Experiments with New-Type Modern Language Tests*. As the editors of the volume acknowledged: "Professor Wood's

ELEANOR PERRY WOOD

This camera study of Ben D. Wood shows him as he appeared in the early 1950's. The photographer was his wife, Eleanor Perry Wood.

three studies open a field of inquiry of great importance and indicate results which are fundamental for modern language testing. The total number of returns involved—for the Regents experiment, 31,025; and for the junior high school surveys, approximately 50,000 —dwarfs by comparison every previous experiment with new-type tests in the modern languages."[13]

As a director of educational research Ben Wood has developed, and has encouraged and helped to develop, several important predictive examinations. The Committee on Graduate Examination that inaugurated the Graduate Record Examination relied heavily upon Wood's advice and assistance. He helped to improve the New York State dental examinations and prepared new tests for the New York Police Academy. Wood helped to inaugurate state educational testing programs in Georgia and Texas, and contributed to the success of testing programs in other states. The National League of Nursing Education received aid from Wood in preparing its tests of nursing proficiency. The American Institute of Accountants asked Wood in 1943 to develop a test for college graduates to predict success in public accounting. Wood spent five years and $100,000 constructing and verifying a battery of tests which was reported to predict success in an accounting career with a high degree of accuracy. Not the least important of Wood's contributions to test development was his indefatigable effort in helping others find aid and financial support for useful projects. For example, he was instrumental in getting funds for Øyvind Skard's adaptation and translation of American tests, which led to a general reorientation of examinations in Norway and throughout the Scandinavian countries.[14]

The Pennsylvania Study

HE MOST AMBITIOUS and important research project with which Wood was associated as director of the Columbia Bureau of Collegiate Educational Research was the Pennsylvania Study, sponsored and financed by the Carnegie Foundation from 1928 to 1932. This study had its inception in a series of discussions at meetings of the College Presidents Association of Pennsylvania during the year 1925-1926. These discussions raised important questions about the relation between secondary schools and colleges and about the best methods for identifying and training college preparatory students. To investigate such mutual problems of colleges and secondary schools, the College Presidents Association, in cooperation with the Pennsylvania State Department of Public Instruction, decided to initiate a state-wide study. It presented a proposal to the Carnegie Foundation with a request for financial assistance.[1]

After several months of negotiations and counterproposals, the Carnegie Foundation agreed to undertake the Pennsylvania Study with William S. Learned as director. Ben Wood was invited to join the project as technical adviser, but the general design as well as the technical details became a thorough mixture of Learned and Wood. As Learned wrote to Wood after the completion of the study: "But much as the study owes you from a technical point of view, your share in the educational aspect of it has far outweighed it. Here you've enlarged, strengthened and steadied the philosophy at so many points, that, except for mere wording, it is as much your argument as mine."[2]

The investigation which Learned and Wood initiated in the spring of 1928 consisted of two parts. The least ambitious part was a twelve-hour comprehensive examination administered to 4,580 graduating seniors in 49 Pennsylvania colleges. This battery of achievement tests presumably measured the accumulated intellectual capital of the class of 1928. The directors called it "an academic inventory of the baccalaureate mind." The second part, designed to measure the academic growth of the baccalaureate mind, was a battery of tests administered to the graduating seniors of 1928 of the public and private secondary schools of Pennsylvania. That portion of the 27,000 seniors who continued their education within the state were tested again in 1930 and in 1932. Approximately 90 per cent of the public high school seniors in the State, 50 per cent of the private school seniors, and 90 per cent of the college seniors participated in the first testing in May 1928. One enthusiastic school superintendent described the study as the most exciting educational adventure imaginable. Most of the school teachers and college faculties of Pennsylvania cooperated with the investigation with similar enthusiasm.[3]

Some of the results of the Pennsylvania Study were reported by the directors through slide lectures at educational conferences and in journal articles while the investigation was in progress. Not until 1938 was the mass of data processed and the final report ready for publication. *The Student and His Knowledge,* Bulletin No. 29 of the Carnegie Foundation for the Advancement of Teaching, written by William S. Learned with Ben Wood listed as junior author, received wide acclaim. Lewis M. Terman, professor of psychology at Stanford University, in a review in the *Journal of Higher Education,* called it "one of the most important contributions thus far made to the problems of higher education in the United States; in the reviewer's opinion, it is the most important since Abraham Flexner's memorable report more than a quarter-century ago on medical education. . . . The authors have set the stage for a thoroughgoing reform of collegiate education."[4] For the next couple of years, until the war absorbed the whole attention of American educators, the report was widely reviewed and volubly discussed.

Like the early muckraking articles on civic affairs at the turn of the century, *The Student and His Knowledge* said little that informed people did not know already. However, it did state the case more accurately and dramatically than ever before. It demonstrated the enormous differences between colleges which granted the same degrees and the even greater differences between students within each college. It applied only to Pennsylvania, but presumably Pennsylvania was a typical state. The situation might even be worse elsewhere. The highest scoring students in several of the colleges ranked below the lowest scorers in other colleges. Yet both groups of institutions would send teachers, engineers, businessmen, and chemists into society with the same ticket of admission. Their transcripts of course credits might even be identical.

The report dramatically exposed the weakness of the course-credit system as a measure of educational achievement. As Dr. Terman noted in his review: "The authors show that in any given subject the correlation between knowledge possessed and units of credit in the subject is unbelievably low. In the social sciences, especially, it is possible to accumulate credits without knowledge or knowledge without credits. In the face of such facts the prevailing course-credit system is not only indefensible, it is ridiculous." This opinion was shared by the authors of the report, who proposed that the course-credit or "time spent" system be replaced by tested achievement as the basis for graduation.

The Learned and Wood investigation also produced disturbing conclusions about teacher trainees in Pennsylvania colleges. The test scores of prospective teachers on the eve of graduation were sometimes lower than the scores of the high school seniors, the level at which many of the college seniors expected to teach. Fifteen per cent of the high school science students, for example, had science test scores superior to the science test scores of nearly 40 per cent of the comparable college seniors who intended to teach. As the report concluded, "we find pupils at the level where these teachers will work surpassing them on their own territory." The average total scores of prospective teachers was consistently lower than those of librarians, journalists, premedical and prelaw students, and engineers. The education majors ranked just above agricultural and secretarial majors.[5]

The Pennsylvania Study was a valuable undertaking. It publicized individual and institutional differences and set a new standard for meaningful educational research. The *Student and His Knowledge* was extremely useful in calling attention to the limitations of the course-credit system of academic bookkeeping. That the situation which it so dramatically exposed is still largely with us only emphasizes the lag between exposure and action in educational reform. "We still have colleges that regularly graduate classes that in ordinary high school English reading and vocabulary tests average at the senior high school level, although there are many colleges whose freshmen stand entirely above the whole population of some of these low colleges," Wood wrote in 1964.[6]

The Pennsylvania Study also had an impact on the testing and guidance movement. The tests administered in 1930 to the Pennsylvania college sophomores demonstrated the usefulness of testing at that level for college guidance purposes. It inspired the American Council on Education to support the proposal of Ben Wood as director of the Cooperative Test Service to inaugurate shortly thereafter a nationwide college sophomore testing program. The Pennsylvania Study also publicized cumulative record keeping. It led directly to the Public School Demonstration Project in Educational Guidance, a five-year (1934-1939) pilot effort to recast the thinking of administrators and teachers about testing and the keeping of cumulative records. Finally, the scoring problems encountered in the Pennsylvania Study led ultimately to the development of the IBM test scoring machine, which was an educational revolution in itself.[7]

The Doctrine of Individualized Education

HE IDEAL of an education fitted to the needs and capacities of individual students has a long history in western educational thought. It rests upon the recognition of individual differences, and educational thinkers from Plato to John Dewey have called attention to the varied interests and learning capacities of human beings. The early years of the twentieth century saw a quickening of interest in this kind of education among American educators, due in large part to the growing emphasis on child-centered education and to the development of new testing devices for measuring individuals. By the early 1920's several American educators were searching for practical ways to make the schools more responsive to individual needs. Eugene Randolph Smith, organizer and headmaster of the Park School of Baltimore, was talking and writing about the need for studying individual characteristics and habits and for keeping an analytical record of students.[1] The original founders of the Progressive Education Association in 1919, among them Smith, Stanwood Cobb, a professor at the United States Naval Academy, and Anne E. George, directress of the Washington Montessori Schools, were also thinking along these lines.[2] Thus, the ideal of individualized education was very much in the air when Ben Wood began to form his own pedagogical ideas.

Wood was attracted to the ideal of individualized education. His unorthodox educational background doubtlessly made him especially receptive to an educational philosophy that recognized individual differences. He had also read John Dewey's books and was impressed by them, especially by *The Child and the Curriculum,* which Dewey had published in Chicago in 1902. In a letter to Dewey in 1935 Wood acknowledged that the thesis of that book had provided an inspiration for his own writings on guidance. He summarized that thesis by quoting a sentence from Dewey's book: "The child is the starting point, the center, and the end. It is he and not the subject matter that determines the quality and quantity of learning." Wood made his career one continuous effort to implement this ideal of child-centered and individualized education.[3]

The philosophy of education expressed by John Dewey and others had become widely accepted by the mid 1930's, but Wood doubted that it had been very widely implemented. "As I survey the schools more than a quarter of a century after you wrote these sentences," he wrote to Dewey, "I find that the child is still neither the starting point, nor the center, nor the end of our educational organization. So far as my observation goes, this is true even in the so-called progressive schools to some extent at least, since all of them start with a predetermined curriculum, and most, if not all of them, seek to apply one uniform standard of achievement."[4] Wood hoped that his own work with comparable tests and cumulative records would encourage a wider implementation of the philosophy which Dewey represented. "I think I am inclined to agree with you in what you say about so-called progressive schools," Dewey replied. "They have, it seems to me, gone much further in setting up a general concept of adaptation of the individual than they have in developing methods for finding out about the abilities, needs and interests of the individual. I am sure that the work you are doing is very helpful in the latter direction."[5]

Wood accepted as an article of faith that the school existed for the individual child and not the other way around. He wrote in 1934 that the highest duty of the school "is not to teach subject matters, but to help develop individual boys and girls of all types into better and happier citizens."[6] Wood subscribed to this central tenet of progressivism in education, but it is not very helpful to describe him as a progressive educator. He actively supported many of the objectives of the progressive movement, but also criticized much that was done in its name. Sometimes he drew fire simultaneously from conservative educators and from teachers colleges which claimed to be progressive.

On one point especially Wood appeared staunchly conservative. He stressed the importance of basic factual knowledge. Wood was a persistent critic of the point of view that gained an ascendancy in some of the teachers colleges that children could be taught to think

IFOR THOMAS

*Ben D. Wood's entire career has focused on efforts to implement in
every way the ideal of child-centered and individualized education.*

without being burdened with "mere facts." He attacked that point
of view in 1936 as co-author of an article published in the *Teachers
College Record.* The article contended that thinking in a factual
vacuum was an absurd impossibility. "From the dull, pedestrian
records of history this point emerges: the immortal tapers of creative
thought were lighted not by any magic of the classroom, but by a
spark of fact impinging upon a well-furnished mind."[7] Wood explained to Charles Swain Thomas of the Harvard Graduate School

of Education, who had highly praised the article, that he had decided to write it "because there has been so much unchallenged propaganda, not in favor of thinking, but against knowledge and information. I am all for progressive education, but I am trying to save progressive education from the lunatic fringe that has put it in a bad light with friends as well as enemies of the movement."[8]

The progressive educators wrote and said a great deal about adjustment. So did Ben Wood. Yet he, significantly, placed the emphasis on the adjustment of the curriculum and the teaching situation to the child rather than the adjustment of the child to the social environment of a classroom oriented around the traditional and prescribed curriculum. Wood was less concerned about adjustment psychology than about curriculum adjustment and the administrative reorganization of the schools. These were essential points in his philosophy of education, and it was these very points which conservatives and some progressives were reluctant to accept. The idea of individualized education, as Wood conceived it, was revolutionary in its implications, and most school administrators and teachers, even in the progressive 1930's, were not revolutionaries.

In an address to the Institute for Student Personnel Workers in June 1925, Wood outlined the first requirement for individualized education. Teachers must know their students thoroughly. "Not only the colleges, but the schools, from kindergarten to university, must realize that their first duty is not to *teach* but to *learn* students. To get accurate and significant information about students, and to record it in a way that will be available and meaningful and directive at each step in the educational ladder, is a duty fully coordinate with, and certainly prerequisite to the proper discharge of the duty to teach students." He compared teaching to the medical profession. Nine-tenths of a successful doctor's work is his diagnosis of the patient's illness. If his diagnosis is accurate, he can usually cure the patient. So it should be with educational guidance.[9]

The success of educational diagnosis depended, Wood thought, on the effective use of two devices: comparable tests systematically used and a cumulative record file. "We cannot hope to do this well by taking instantaneous snapshots such as we get by the usual college entrance intelligence and content examinations and interviews; we must have complete and continuous cumulative records of defined capacities, achievements and interests, expressed in objective and comparable units from the kindergarten to the university."[10] To use tests in that way, not to assign a grade, but to construct a cumulative profile of a student's knowledge, was unusual and highly unorthodox.

"It is difficult for us today to realize how narrow were the ideas of both testing and guidance, prevalent as of 1934," Wood recently remarked.[11] A test was then regarded as a unique experience: a single event never to be repeated. It was a snapshot that revealed at a fixed moment in time the quantity and perhaps something of the quality of a student's knowledge. As the purpose of a test was usually to determine how much knowledge a student had acquired, its logical place was at the end of a unit of instruction. On the basis of test results, teachers assigned class marks, committees awarded scholarships, and colleges admitted freshman classes. It was nearly the civil service philosophy of examination, establishing a merit system for the distribution of academic patronage. The new objective tests were introduced and used during their first years essentially to accomplish this older purpose more efficiently and more accurately. Tests were primarily administrative devices that came after the teaching was finished.

It was as diagnostic devices in the service of individualized instruction that Wood saw the greatest potential for the objective tests. They were admirably suited for compiling a continuous record of a student's development. The performance of that function would also give the testing movement a new sense of purpose and direction, which Wood thought it badly needed. "While there has been much room for technical improvement," he said in 1934, "the chief defect in the testing movement has been the neglect of building an adequate philosophy and system of using test results for effective and constructive educational guidance in the larger sense of that term."[12] Or as he has said recently: "The thing that made the testing movement so unpalatable was that the people who used tests had no philosophy of education, and testing became the whole thing."[13] To enlist the testing movement in the cause of individualized education required a revolutionary change in the prevailing ideas about using tests.

By testing at the beginning or in the middle of a unit of instruction, or by having a file of previous test results at hand at the outset, a teacher could diagnose the weaknesses of his students early and adapt his teaching accordingly. Testing would become a matter of continuous measurement helpful to the student and teacher alike. The result would be a continuous record of a student's progress in the mastery of subject matter and intellectual skills from kindergarten to the university. As he ascended the educational ladder, the student would become better known instead of becoming increasingly more of a stranger to his teachers. "According to this conception," Wood wrote, "the highest purpose and ultimate aim of the objective testing movement is not to make better college entrance or course-credit examinations, but to help inaugurate a continuous study of individuals throughout the whole educational ladder by means of systematically recorded comparable measures and observations which will make such spasmodic examinations largely unnecessary, or at most, only an addition to the growing record of a growing individual."[14]

Requisite to this proposed use of tests was the systematic keeping of records. The records would serve the teachers as charts of a student's actual achievement and growth and would serve the educational system as a more meaningful common currency than the traditional course-credits. For the test records to serve either function adequately, an efficient, widely accepted, and standardized record form was essential. This problem was largely solved in 1928 by the adoption of a standard record form by the American Council on Education. It had been designed by a subcommittee headed by Ben Wood. He regards the original American Council record form as a major breakthrough for individualized education — "the greatest single thing I have ever done."[15] As an indication of the broadness of Wood's concept of guidance, about four-fifths of the record form was reserved for data other than test scores. Wood thinks it is essential for the teacher to know about the student's nonacademic interests. To know a student thoroughly, he has said, a teacher must know "what the individual thinks about when he isn't thinking about anything in particular."[16]

The increasing use of standardized tests and cumulative records by the late 1930's also suggested to Wood the feasibility of a dual marking system. The test data would serve as one set of school "marks," a set expressed in universally recognized units. That would free the local marking system for whatever moral and equitable purposes the local school system might choose. There would be no danger in confusing an "A" for effort with an "A" for achievement. "What I am proposing is a dual system of marks, because in effect we are here concerned with two related but independent purposes, both of which are important and neither of which should be or need be sacrificed for the other. For certification and transfer purposes, comparable measures are indispensable. . . . For the moral, social, and disciplinary welfare of the individual pupil, the local school marks will rate the pupil in terms of his achievement of goals and standards that are considered appropriate to him." The local marks would be reported only to the parents; the standardized test marks would be reserved for employers and college admission officers. Wood proposed this scheme as a possible method of making school grades universally meaningful without having to overcome the social pressures that were the principal obstacle to such a needed reform.[17]

Supplanting the snapshot theory of testing with the diagnostic, moving picture idea was only part of the requirement for individualizing education. Wood believed that the prescribed and uniform curriculum was an obstacle equally great. The very idea of a single curriculum, he contends, is incompatible with the fact of individual differences. "It is like the doctors meeting once a year to prescribe the regimen for all the hospitals for the year to come."[18] In recent years he has given an increasing amount of thought to curriculum reform. His thoughts today about the curriculum are as radical as were his ideas about testing in the 1920's.

In Wood's ideal school of the future "specific school curriculum requirements will be limited to reading, writing (by shorthand and touch typing), and the so-called modern mathematics; but these requirements will be emphasized and pursued (never *enforced*), only so far as the inborn ability and present level of achievement of the *individual* child will permit without producing traumatic results or provoking resentment by too difficult or too rapid assignments. Beyond these basic and justifiable pursuits for all children, the curriculum will be simply a free library from which each student shall choose according to his own abilities, interests and needs, with such guidance and leadership as the teachers may offer without anything approaching enforcement or coercion of any kind."[19]

"I have been told that this idealistic plan will not work; but I feel sure it will work well for perhaps 98 per cent of normal children. I am sure it would be more successful than our present prison-like methods of control and enforcement, which centuries of school experience in every land have demonstrated to be a howling failure for large proportions of our children over and beyond the increasing numbers who become delinquents, outright criminals, total or functional illiterates, or those who are born with sub-moronic mental ability. I am not, and never have been, a 'progressive' who shirks the need for maintaining discipline, but the authoritarian, autocratic, judgmental methods that still characterize most schools are obvious failures for the very children who most need genuine help in developing self-discipline."[20]

The ideas that Wood expressed above in 1964 were foreshadowed in much that he wrote during the 1930's and before. He has ever maintained that "coercion in education may be as dangerous as legalized intolerance in religion." Included in his definition of coercion is the requirement that all school children submit to a uniform curriculum, which he regards as a form of intolerance reminiscent of the Spanish Inquisition. "Even if some do learn the prescribed minimum under the pressure of remedial treatment," he wrote 30 years ago, "the results may not be worth the effort. Indeed, if we consider the attitudes of despair, the feelings of inferiority, the habits of dependence, the frequently temporary and superficial character of forced learning, and the loss of opportunity and time for learning something that is within the comprehension of the pupil, it is by no means certain that the efforts to 'remedy' children up to prescribed minimum are not positively harmful. . . . Concretely, we should acknowledge that however essential scheduled teaching may be for the mass of our population, there are some pupils who would become more valuable citizens if they had less rather than more teaching, if they spent less rather than more time in the orthodox classroom, if they had less interference from teachers and tutors and more time for reading, for learning, and for self-initiated and self-propelled thinking."[21]

Wood believes that no small part of the responsibility for the traditionally high rate of academic failure and dropout in the United States rests upon the failure of the educational system to cope with individual differences. We have tried to force a uniform curriculum upon a heterogeneous school population and have been notoriously unsuccessful. He insists that a high rate of academic failure is not a necessary corollary to a public, compulsory educational system. "The duty of publicly supported educational institutions, especially those that operate under the compulsory attendance law, is to help all pupils, whether they be geniuses, mediocrities, or morons. To fail large masses of young people on the ground that they have not lived up to the minimum essentials of a predetermined curriculum is both a professional blunder and a social injustice." An alternative does exist: to fit the curriculum more nearly to the abilities and needs of individuals.[22]

Wood also suspects that binding students to a uniform and teacher-dominated regimen during their school years tends to eradicate creative genius. It may clamp more tightly upon the student's mind an orthodox mold of thought which he otherwise might have broken through to an original and creative idea. The Curtiss flying machine, Wood points out, was theoretically perfect according to the orthodox academic principles of aerodynamics of its time. But it would not fly. The solution to the problem of manned flight did not come from the schools, but was worked out by the Wright brothers tinkering in a bicycle shop. Wood refers to Thomas Alva Edison as another case in point. The great inventor was advised to quit school at a young age because the state despaired of ever teaching him anything. So Edison dropped out. "That was probably the most brilliant piece of guidance work in the history of education, and completely by accident," Wood says. "Had Edison been subjected to the typically prescribed tropisms of the classroom, every bit of his creative energy would probably have been crushed. What we've got to do is to help the Edisons develop their creative genius inside the schools."[23]

Another essential requirement for individualizing education is the breaking of the administrative lockstep of the graded school. "One of the things I have often advocated is the nongraded school," Wood says, "which has now received considerable support in a few schools in this country, especially the one in Melbourne, Florida, and the Decatur-Lakeview High School in Illinois."[24] Implicit in all that Wood has written about individualized education is the assumption that a student's progress through the school system should be governed solely by his rate of achievement. The purpose of the school is to educate the child; it does not exist to fulfill administrative requirements. The student's level of attainment should be judged by his cumulative record of test scores, not by the amount of time served at an artificial grade level. Like several other reforms that Wood has proposed, this one depends upon substituting cumulative test records for the course-credit system.

Wood has long recognized the traditional teacher-dominated classroom as another obstacle to individualization. The authoritarian and teacher-dominated learning situation is a medieval idea which Wood considers one of the most persistent and durable fallacies in the educational tradition of the western world. We all admit as a general principle, verified over and over in the course of our lives, that we learn most thoroughly when we think things through and work things out for ourselves. Then nothing could be more reasonable, Wood contends, than the proposition that correct teaching is that which increases the opportunities for self-learning. Besides, only such a shift of emphasis in the classroom will free the teacher for his proper role of aiding individuals to learn. Individualized instruction is only possible in a classroom designed for individualized learning. As Wood wrote in 1936: "Nothing less than basic changes in the fundamental philosophy and administration of our schools, and nothing less than a complete reorientation of our teachers regarding the hierarchy of their duties, will suffice to realize the ideals of educational and vocational guidance. The basic changes required are clearly implied in the justly famous statement of Professor Henry C. Morrison to the effect that teachers should spend half their time studying their pupils as growing individuals, and the rest of their time doing what that study indicates is desirable and necessary."[25]

The Educational Records Bureau

HERE were several indications of progress toward individualized education by the late 1920's. One was the adoption by the American Council on Education of the cumulative record form. No less important was the almost immediate acceptance of the Educational Records Bureau, founded in 1927, of which Ben Wood became director in 1933.

The Bureau, as originally proposed in 1927, was the brain child of Charles K. Taylor, one of the most ebullient personalities in education at that time and a promoter extraordinary. Taylor sold the idea of a central testing bureau, which he said had occurred to him while in the Army in France during the First World War, to the headmasters of several Eastern private schools and to the Keith Foundation. His original plan was to distribute and score intelligence tests to aid schools in judging the fitness of their pupils for college entrance. In the early stages of drumming up support for his proposal, Taylor paid a visit to Dean Hawkes and Ben Wood and asked for their assistance. They began by acquainting him with the cumulative record form, then almost ready for publication, and its underlying philosophy of continuous guidance. After extended discussions with Dean Hawkes, Eugene R. Smith, John A. Lester, and other educational leaders who were convinced that guidance was essential to education, Taylor agreed to broaden his original plan to include achievement and other tests and other kinds of information useful for guidance, and to extend the service from the senior high school level downward as far as group testing might be feasible.[1]

Wood was preoccupied with a dozen other projects, including the production of the Pennsylvania College Achievement Tests, but he recognized the potential of the expanded plan for the Bureau and helped to persuade Eleanor Perry Wood to take on the task of putting the plan into operation. The new agency began operation on October 1, 1927, with a staff of two and an active membership of four schools.

The warm reception of the Educational Records Bureau far exceeded the expectation of the director and almost overwhelmed the new agency's resources. Within a year the membership had increased to 28. When the fall testing program was added in 1931—achievement and aptitude tests for diagnostic purposes—the membership was 216 schools. It increased steadily thereafter, except for the period of the Second World War. By 1964 the Educational Records Bureau included 925 educational institutions, including public and private schools and colleges.[2]

The Educational Records Bureau (ERB) has encouraged schools to keep cumulative records of student development. It was originally designed to serve as the central record bank of its member schools. According to Hart Fessenden of the Fessenden School, "One of the original selling points of the ERB was that boys would take these tests, they would be corrected, scores sent the schools, etc., and a record made on the boy's card in New York. We had a card here, too. After each series of tests the cards would go to New York and would be filled out there and sent back to us. The theory was that school X, wanting information about a boy, would write the ERB to ask for it. The rather advanced thinking was that this record would supply the secondary school with enough information to accept or reject a boy."[3] In time, the traffic in cards became too heavy and too expensive, and the schools were asked to keep their own records on forms supplied by the Bureau.

The record keeping function of the Bureau was somewhat more important in the early years than at present, although the Bureau does keep records of individual results of all tests ever scored at the Bureau for member schools so that it can, on request, prepare a cumulative record for any individual in any member school. In addition to its regular scoring and reporting service, it makes available to its member schools a systematic cumulative record service by special arrangement, and a few schools do take advantage of this service. At present the Bureau also provides general consulting service on test matters for its members; it recommends tests, distributes and scores them; it does continuous research on the results; it provides test norms based on the school populations which it serves;

and it issues publications designed to help school administrators, teachers, counselors, and parents understand and use test results.[4]

Not the least of the contributions which the Educational Records Bureau has made to education under Ben Wood's direction are the annual conferences of its member institutions. As its membership expanded to include most of the important private schools in the East, and an increasing number of high schools and colleges, the annual conferences became educational events of considerable significance. "I believe it is becoming one of the outstanding educational meetings in the country," said President A. D. Henderson of Antioch College in 1937.[5] The speakers at the conference in that year included President James B. Conant of Harvard, President Henderson, Dean Max McConn of Lehigh University, and several other prominent educators. That conference, which marked the tenth anniversary of the Bureau, was also a memorable event for the Woods. They received much praise and congratulation, especially Mrs. Wood, for the Bureau's successful decade.

Eleanor Perry Wood contributed more than any other single individual to the early operating success of the Educational Records Bureau. For many of the schoolmen who used its services, the Bureau was Mrs. Wood. Under her management, the Bureau became financially self-supporting. It has not received any Foundation support since 1931, although it continued to receive rent-free quarters from Columbia University until December 1949. "The Educational Records Bureau, as a functioning organization, was literally the creation of Eleanor Perry Wood," Ben Wood has said. "Dean Hawkes and several of the 'Founding Fathers,' notably Eugene R. Smith and John A. Lester, and I stood by to help her in matters of policy and finance whenever she needed such help; but the planning, staffing, organization and administration of the Bureau were entirely hers from the founding in 1927 until 1936 when we were fortunate in getting Arthur E. Traxler as her associate."[6]

After Mrs. Wood's retirement in 1940 for reasons of health, Ben Wood continued as titular director; but the growth of the Educational Records Bureau and expansion of its services during the following quarter century was in large part the work of Arthur E. Traxler, the executive director. At least half of the 200 research studies published in the annual bulletins of the Bureau were prepared by Traxler, in addition to his books on guidance, summaries of reading research reports, and numberless brochures, articles and reviews.

The Cooperative Test Service

DUCATORS who attempted continuous testing for educational guidance prior to about 1930 quickly encountered a practical problem. There were not enough tests made in multiple and equivalent forms. The Pennsylvania Study, the Educational Records Bureau, and a growing number of continuous guidance programs in secondary schools and colleges were threatened by the lack of suitable tests. Wood said of the Pennsylvania Study in 1931: "Already we are at the end of our program unless new tests are made available because the tests that are now on the market have been used anywhere from two to three or four times in the same institution and the teachers in these schools simply refuse to give those tests anymore. They claim that many of their students have memorized them."[1] Very few tests were constructed with more than two forms at that time. The 20-odd comparable forms of the Thorndike Intelligence Examination for High School Graduates and the five forms of the New Stanford Achievement Test were pioneering ventures still almost alone in the field. To meet this need and to rescue a number of promising educational projects, Ben Wood and the American Council on Education organized the Cooperative Test Service in 1930.

The critical need for comparable tests was brought to the attention of the American Council on Education by its Central Committee on Personnel Procedures. This committee, under the chairmanship of Dean Herbert E. Hawkes, also presented an outline and a favorable recommendation for a test constructing agency. Wood had prepared the outline. The American Council on Education voted to accept the proposal and outline at its executive meeting on October 25, 1930. The new agency, the Cooperative Test Service, would remain a creature of the American Council on Education and was placed under the supervision of Dean Hawkes's committee. It was underwritten by a subvention from the General Education Board of $500,000, the money to be allotted over a period of 10 years. It was hoped that after that time the Cooperative Test Service would have a sufficient income from the sale of tests to function indefinitely as a nonprofit-making but self-supporting enterprise. The American Council on Education appointed Ben D. Wood director of the new agency.[2]

The Cooperative Test Service began operations in Hamilton Hall on the Columbia University campus. This generous subsidy of office space was continued after the testing service moved to more permanent quarters in the University's old medical school building on Amsterdam Avenue, alongside the Educational Records Bureau. Although the two organizations shared connecting buildings and were both under Wood's directorship after 1933, they retained their individuality. The Bureau used many of the Cooperative Tests, but it also constructed its own tests in biology, chemistry, physics, and certain aspects of mathematics, and its member institutions were at liberty to order tests produced by commercial test publishers.[3]

As director of the Cooperative Test Service, Ben Wood utilized the talent of the nation's most experienced and expert test builders. One of the working objectives of the organization was, as E. F. Lindquist phrased it, "to conserve and to utilize effectively the supply of good test-building talent now available in this country." Among the authors of the Cooperative Tests were V. A. C. Henmon of the University of Wisconsin, Donald G. Paterson and F. S. Beers of the University of Minnesota, E. F. Lindquist of the State University of Iowa, Ralph W. Tyler of Ohio State University and several other pioneers in the objective testing movement. The tests were edited and published in New York, but their construction was a national and a cooperative undertaking.[4]

Although the professional competence of the authors would have insured the production of Cooperative Tests of good quality, elaborate precautions were also taken to establish a close correspondence between the tests and the subject matter being taught in the nation's schools. Experts in the various subject matter fields made detailed analyses of the content of school courses and of the most widely used school textbooks. These specialists then wrote the test questions based on the topics and concepts which educational authorities agreed were important and appropriate measurable outcomes of classroom instruction. Before the final publication of Cooperative Tests, all test items were pretested and analyzed statistically to determine their effectiveness. The analysis of student performance on these tests led to the publication of a large number of statistical studies by John C. Flanagan, Statistician and later Associate Director of the Cooperative Test Service, and by staff members Frederick B. Davis and David G. Ryans. They also prepared tables of norms to aid in the interpretation of the tests.[5]

The publication of successive forms of Cooperative Tests not only kept more or less comparable forms coming, but enabled the tests to keep pace with changes in the academic disciplines. Donald J. Shank, Assistant to the President of the American Council on Education from 1935 to 1945, and liaison officer for the Cooperative Test Service program, recalls that "a lot of the tests were way ahead of what was going on in many secondary schools and college classrooms."[6] Maintaining comparability among the various forms was, however, an important and difficult problem. This was largely resolved, or at least greatly simplified, by John C. Flanagan, who developed a Scaled Score system which utilized Truman L. Kelley's 50-point concept.[7] According to Wood, Flanagan's Scaled Score system was "perhaps the most significant original contribution in two decades so far as the practical use of test measures for guidance is concerned."[8]

Under Ben Wood's direction and with the collaboration of many people, a useful set of tests came into existence. "The Cooperative Tests are probably the most useful battery of achievement tests now available for the secondary school and college on a national basis," wrote Arthur Traxler, Executive Director of the Educational Records Bureau, in 1939.[9] They became widely used. By 1933 almost 300,000 tests had been distributed and the annual increment thereafter was about 20 per cent. Annual sales passed the million mark in the year ending June 30, 1938. "The total distribution to date," the director noted in June 1940, "is nearly 6,000,000 Cooperative Tests and nearly 1,000,000 answer sheets. The most significant feature of this distribution is that a large fraction represents the same schools and colleges year after year, and that an increasing number of these purchasers are using the tests systematically for guidance purposes."[10]

As the construction of Cooperative Tests proceeded and became systematic, Wood gave an increasing amount of his time to educating school administrators and teachers on the proper use of tests and cumulative records for continuous guidance. In this educational work Wood had the full support of the Committee on Personnel Methods of the American Council on Education. The Cooperative Test Service was part of a coordinated effort of the committee to introduce more effective measurement and guidance practices in the nation's schools. It had begun a multiple attack on the problem which included sponsoring the American Council on Education's Psychological Examination, prepared by Professor and Mrs. L. L. Thurstone, and the adoption of the cumulative record form. The members of the committee recognized that the success of all their efforts depended upon the acceptance by administrators and teachers of a proper philosophy of guidance.[11]

". . . the first and most difficult task of the guidance movement is to make itself understood by the mass of teachers, and to demonstrate the compatibility of its philosophy and methodology with the highest ideals of education—intellectual, moral, and physical," Wood had written.[12] This was the educational task that Wood took upon himself. By the mid-1930's he was spending as much time on the road as in his office. He traveled throughout the country speaking to meetings of headmasters associations, to associations of college presidents and college registrars, to the faculty and students of teachers colleges, to school teachers, and to parents and citizens groups. His effectiveness in explaining the role of tests and cumulative records in educational guidance can be judged from the correspondence that came into his New York office from all parts of the country. "You have completely sold the guidance and testing idea to the Mount Hermon faculty," wrote a school administrator from Mount Hermon, Massachusetts. A college registrar in Wisconsin wrote that Wood's appearance there "was not merely inspiring. It will have undoubted effect upon the organization of the educational program in this state." From Skidmore College, President Henry T. Moore wrote to Wood that he was greatly impressed by "the many evidences of the deep influence your researches are having on college education." Wood had an impact on almost every level of the educational system.[13]

The educational program was only one aspect of Wood's contribution to the educational measurement and guidance movement in the United States. He also helped to organize state and local testing and guidance programs, and on many occasions the Cooperative Test Service furnished the test materials for these programs without cost.[14] Wood also participated in the Eight-Year Study of the Progressive Education Association as a member of the Commission on the Relation of School and College and of the Committee on Evaluation and Recording.[15] He contributed several articles on guidance to educational journals and co-authored a book entitled *Measuring and Guiding Individual Growth*.[16] Primarily at Wood's suggestion and urging, the American Council on Education published two influential books on educational measurement: *The Construction and Use of Achievement Examinations* (1936), edited by Herbert E. Hawkes, E. F. Lindquist, and C. R. Mann, and *Educational Measurement* (1951), edited by E. F. Lindquist. The editor acknowledged in the Preface to the latter book: "This volume might well be regarded as a monument to Dr. Wood's outstanding leadership in educational measurement in this country during the past three decades."[17]

From time to time the Cooperative Test Service also made special tests for noneducational institutions and for other than guidance purposes. It worked with such professional organizations as the American Chemical Society and the American Home Economics Association and with various departments of the United States government. The Cooperative Test Service also made the first three forms of the highly successful scholarship examination introduced in 1937 by the College Entrance Examination Board. This was done on a temporary emergency basis until the College Board was able to continue the work by itself. The noneducational work of the Cooperative Test Service assumed major importance during the Second World War. Several of its tests were requisitioned by the military, including the whole of the 1940 edition of the National Teacher Examinations. The latter was used to examine candidates for officer training schools and was said to be the only suitable battery of tests in existence for use with persons mature enough to be officer candidates. Among the wartime projects to which the Cooperative Test Service contributed were the testing programs of the United States Armed Forces Institute and the Naval College Training Program. It also sent three of its highly trained specialists into the war as commissioned officers, where they developed new tests for classification purposes and helped to direct large-scale testing programs.

Ben Wood resigned as director of the Cooperative Test Service in 1945 because of ill health. Two years later the American Council on Education agreed to combine its testing facilities with those of the College Entrance Examination Board and the Carnegie Foundation for the Advancement of Teaching to form the Educational

Testing Service. At the end of 1947 the Cooperative Test Service became the Cooperative Test Division of ETS. The function which the Cooperative Test Service performed for American education was perhaps best summarized by William S. Learned of the Carnegie Foundation. "In my judgment the significant thing about the Cooperative Test Service is that it incorporates in impressive style an exceedingly important idea—an idea that is fundamental to the far-reaching transformation that is now going on in all American education. It is not a question of popularizing certain devices but rather one of educating faculties and administrators to the effective use of all instruments for measurement as they are steadily improved. Certainly no one in this country has been more active in defining, guiding and interpreting this movement than Ben Wood has been. He has performed a really monumental service."[18]

Education and Technology

THROUGHOUT his career Ben D. Wood has been alert to the new possibilities opened to education by the technological revolution of the present century. Few educators have contributed as significantly as he to the wedding of these two civilizing forces. He has been among the first to suggest and to explore the educational usefulness of mechanical devices ranging from the motion picture projectors and portable typewriters of the 1920's to closed-circuit television and the learning machines of the 1960's.

In an address before the Harvard Teachers Association in 1931, Ben Wood cautioned his audience against what seemed to be the ingrained, anti-mechanical prejudice of American teachers. He spoke in defense of *homo faber*. "I cannot see how the restoration of the ox cart and the mud highway, or the substitution of the Dutch oven for the electric or gas range could possibly make better travelers or happier homemakers." Yet he had encountered scores of teachers who shut the industrial revolution out of the classroom on the grounds that mechanical contraptions detracted from good teaching. He concluded his speech with the reminder that any machine that released a teacher's mind and energies from routine chores to permit a larger amount of individual instruction properly belonged in the equipment of education.[1]

While Wood has helped to publicize and to promote almost every kind of mechanical teaching aid, he has been most closely associated with the development of teaching films, the typewriter as a learning device, and the electronic test scoring machine.

The potential of motion pictures as visual teaching aids was virtually unexplored until the 1920's. Although the larger school systems owned projectors and rented films, they invariably showed the films in the school auditorium as entertainment or for the purpose of general education. The few classroom film experiments that were undertaken had been conducted with small groups of children under rather artificial classroom conditions. No one had attempted to study the accumulative effect of films used over a considerable period of time in a normal classroom situation.[2]

The value of motion pictures used as ordinary teaching aids was suggested in 1922 by the newly established committee on visual education of the National Education Association. In subsequent years the committee discussed the question with representatives of the motion picture industry, but the lack of data about the value of teaching films kept the joint conferences from being very fruitful. The industry was reluctant to invest money in an uncertain product.

To find out the practical value of educational films, George Eastman announced in 1926 that the Eastman Kodak Company would sponsor at its expense an experiment in the use of classroom films. By that time Ben Wood's reputation as an educational researcher was well established, and a representative of the Eastman Company consulted with him about the design of the experiment. The company was impressed with his general proposal and invited Wood to become co-director of the experiment. His associate was Frank N. Freeman of the University of Chicago.[3]

The teaching film experiment conducted by Wood and Freeman from February to May of 1928 utilized twenty teaching films integrated into two 12-week units in geography and general science. It involved nearly 11,000 students and 200 teachers, in grade levels four to nine, in 12 cities in widely separated areas of the United States. The films and the textbooks for these units were designed especially for this experiment. In each city a control group was also selected—students who were taught with the same printed materials but without the motion pictures. The teachers of the control groups were encouraged to use any other kind of visual aid that seemed appropriate. The relative effectiveness of the two methods of instruction was measured by objective tests. A comprehensive examination was administered to all the students at the beginning of the experiment and another at the end. Tests of a more specific nature were given at the end of each topic covered in the film series.

The report of the 1928 film experiment, entitled *Motion Pictures in the Classroom,* is a classic in the literature of educational visual aids. In the first place the authors concluded that motion pictures had an enormous potential as classroom aids. They predicted that the educational film would rival the entertainment film in its impact upon American social life. The report also provided sound advice on the use of films as visual aids. The authors emphasized that films would have substantial pedagogical value only if carefully integrated into the routine activity of the classroom. "The casual introduction of films into the curriculum without careful organization is of comparatively little value. Insofar as possible, a classroom film should always be used for some definite and particular purpose. It should be a necessary link in the chain of development of the subject. It should constitute the necessary basis for the understanding, by the pupil, of the phases of the topic which follow, and a clarifying of those that have preceded."[4]

The directors tried to find out the precise nature of the films' contribution to learning as well as to assess their general effectiveness. They discovered that the groups exposed to the films scored higher than the control groups both on conceptual-type items and on descriptive-type items. Apparently the more precise notions about geography and science which the students got from the films' physical description also tended to promote exactness and soundness in their more abstract thinking about these subjects. In the years to come, Wood would develop in greater detail the idea that precise factual information is inseparable from precise thinking. As for the general effectiveness of the films: "If we examine the average gains made by the entire group of children in all cities and on all topics taken together, we find that the X group excelled the C group by a substantial and significant margin."[5]

The results of the Wood and Freeman study undoubtedly influenced George Eastman's decision to embark upon the production of educational films. He was also urged to do so by two young and energetic employees, Edward Peck Curtis, later a Major General in the Army, and Marion Bayard Folsom, who became Secretary of Health, Education, and Welfare in 1955. Through a subsidiary corporation called Eastman Classroom Films, the Eastman Kodak company produced several hundred silent classroom films. This venture, conducted by the company at a substantial loss, primed the pump for the deluge of educational films that has followed.[6]

The Wood and Freeman experiment has another and perhaps even greater significance. Its design was a trial blueprint for the classroom of the future. It suggested a rationally constructed learning situation based upon a successful integration of mechanical teaching aids, textbook materials, and sequential tests for measuring progress. It was a radical departure from the current practice of 1928. If the average classroom of the 1960's still falls short of that highly imaginative design, it is perhaps an indication that Ben Wood on that occasion was more than 30 years ahead of the times.

THE TYPEWRITER AS A LEARNING DEVICE

Ben Wood and Frank N. Freeman undertook a second collaboration in educational research the year following the teaching film study. This was their pioneering study of the typewriter as a learning aid in kindergarten and elementary school. The investigation was supported over a three-year period by the four principal manufacturers of portable typewriters in the United States and was administered by a specially created, independent Typewriter Educational Research Bureau. The companies were interested in opening a new market for their product, but Wood and Freeman designed and undertook the experiment solely to investigate the pedagogical possibilities of mechanical writing devices. As they said in their published report: "It cannot be too much emphasized that we are concerned with an educational investigation and not an investigation of typewriting as an end in itself. The typewriter has been studied as an instrument in the performance of activities already required by the existing curriculum, not as an instrument in a new course of study."[7] The two-hundred-page report, burdened with the cumbersome title *An Experimental Study of the Educational Influences of the Typewriter in the Elementary School Classroom,* ranks alongside the books of Maria Montessori as a classic of kindergarten and elementary education. It is a fascinating book.

The design of the typewriter experiment was similar to that of the previous Wood and Freeman study. Over 12,000 pupils from kindergarten through the sixth grade took part in the study, representing eight public school systems and five private schools in eight cities in the United States. They were equally divided into experimental and control groups. Among the 6,125 experimental students, the directors apportioned the 1,839 portable typewriters which the companies had loaned to them, a ratio of about two machines for each seven pupils. The teachers of the experimental classrooms were given complete freedom in integrating the typewriters into their normal classroom routine. As a result, the time which pupils from various classrooms spent at the machines varied, but the learning situation was kept as natural as possible. The time at the machine for each pupil totaled 50 to 80 minutes per week in kindergarten and 90 to 130 minutes per week in the remaining grades. The teachers of both the experimental and the control groups were asked to save all the written work of every pupil with the single exception of arithmetic papers. The written work served as an important part of the experimental data. Supplementary data was provided by achievement tests and reports from the teachers about individual reactions to the machines.

The typewriter experiment was such a large undertaking that in the end the directors were able to analyze only a small fraction of the data which it produced. Scoring the several thousand achievement tests that were administered in the beginning and at the end of the experiment was a large task in itself. It did not compare, however, with the problem of analyzing the children's written work, which by the end also included a large volume of arithmetic work. The experimental classes insisted on writing even their arithmetic exercises with the typewriter. Saving every scrap of paper resulted in an appallingly large collection of writings. After studying the sampling problem involved, Wood and Freeman decided to use the material from only four of the cooperating centers: a total of about 578,000 pieces of paper.

After dividing the piles of paper into several categories and comparing the work of the experimental and control classes on a quantitative basis, the directors arrived at several interesting conclusions. Use of the typewriter seemed to encourage original composition. The experimental classes wrote substantially more and longer papers in the category that included stories, letters, and original classroom projects. The number of original writings in the upper grades that exceeded 300 words was 50 per cent larger for the experimental pupils.

The most pronounced effect of the typewriter on volume of writing was registered for the kindergarten and first and second grades. "It appears that the typewriter children in the early grades attempt a greater number of both original and copied writing projects than the control children, and carry these undertakings further."[8] Use of the typewriter also appeared to have a stimulating effect on handwriting. The typewriter classes of the first and second grades did twice as much handwriting as the other children. Although the nature of the written work in the kindergarten classes did not permit a detailed analysis, the effect of the typewriter was pronounced there, also. "While the amount of sense material in these papers is small, the fact of having so many attempts at writing from kindergarten children is highly significant; and the tremendous differences between the average number of attempts of the experimental and control kindergartners indicates that the classroom typewriter has effected a release of childish impulses 'to write.' "9

The most enlightening part of the Wood and Freeman report was the section devoted to teachers' comments. The impressionistic reports of the experimental teachers presented results that were not registered in the objective data. They described the machines' influence on children's attitudes toward learning and on the social and intellectual atmosphere of the classroom. A number of teachers commented about the unusual intensity of interest and amount of self-activity displayed by children at the typewriters. That some of this activity was rather purposeless did not necessarily detract from its value. The directors noted that several of the more experienced teachers, impressed by the self-initiated character of the exercises and by the persistence and interest with which the exercises were carried out, discerned in even the frivolous typing exercises educational values of a high order.

Many of the teachers, especially those in kindergarten and the early grades, reported that the typewriter was instrumental in "bringing out" the shy, noncooperative, and slow pupils. By providing them with something they could do well and something they could compare with objective models, the typewriter helped them to achieve social as well as intellectual release. As one kindergarten teacher commented: "Any new child, bold or shy, discovers the typewriter as a new toy and rejoices in being able to accomplish something. The shy child feels his power and becomes one of the group."10 In doing this, the typewriter also tended to foster an essential condition for learning, the attitude that results from consistently successful endeavor. Writing at the machine, making perfect letters with every stroke, tended to develop that kind of motivation that results from success feeding upon itself. "The *success* he is able to attain with a typewriter is very different and very much greater than with almost any other form of activity in which he engages," a kindergarten teacher remarked.11

Perhaps the most obvious effect of the typewriter was the change it wrought on the organization and atmosphere of the classroom. The presence of the typewriter in the learning situation tended to increase the number of cooperative undertakings, such as the children helping each other to learn to type, to dictate letters, and to compare and judge each other's work. Along with this heightened social and cooperative sense, children tended to develop the habit of self-initiated and self-propelled activity. In other words, the experimental classes became less dependent upon the teacher to the extent that learning became a cooperative effort among themselves. As one kindergarten teacher put it: "The 'goose-step' cannot survive in a typewriter-rhythmed room."[12] "The social atmosphere in the classroom seems to be favorably affected by means of the typewriters," said a third-grade teacher. "It seems to be a very busy place when every child is doing something worthwhile which is of great interest to him. They are anxious to help each other also."[13]

The results of the typewriter experiment sufficiently impressed the teachers who participated in it that 87 per cent recommended the typewriter as standard classroom equipment for their grade level. The directors also concluded that the typewriter had extraordinary value as a learning device. Unfortunately, the typewriter report appeared in 1932, the blackest year of the Great Depression. It was widely hailed as an original and important achievement in educational research, but the innovation which it suggested was rejected as economically unfeasible. Ben Wood still maintains that the pedagogical value of typewriters as early learning devices more than justifies the cost of their installation in the classroom.

TEST SCORING MACHINE

It was apparent to many people in education by the 1930's that the future of large-scale testing programs was limited because of the test scoring problems involved. The hand scoring of test booklets was a slow and expensive process. Wood first encountered the problem during his work with the New York State Regents Examination and faced it again during the Pennsylvania Study. One projected phase of that study had to be discontinued, partly because of the enormous expense involved in scoring tests. In the autumn of 1928, with the Pennsylvania Study under way, Ben Wood wrote to 10 corporations which manufactured computing equipment, explaining the need for a machine to score examinations. Several of the com-

Ben Wood and Thomas J. Watson, Sr., inspect the IBM tabulator that was modified in 1932 to score the Strong Vocational Interest Blank.

panies did not bother to reply, but Thomas J. Watson, Sr., president of International Business Machines Corporation, telephoned Wood and arranged a meeting.

His first meeting with Thomas J. Watson is one of Ben Wood's fondest memories. It marked the beginning of a close, lifelong friendship. Watson was such a busy man that he told Wood when they met at the Century Club that he had only an hour to state his business. A secretary was posted to remind Watson when the time was up. Wood's ideas about the potential uses of machines in education, especially the possibilities of electronic data processing machines (a figment of Wood's imagination at that early date), so appealed to Watson that he kept Wood talking the entire afternoon. Every hour on the hour the secretary was waved away.

Watson was obviously impressed by Ben Wood's fertile and far-ranging imagination. He made Wood a consultant to IBM, with an annual retainer of $5,000, and promised him technical assistance in exploring several of the avenues suggested that day. Shortly thereafter three truckloads of IBM computing equipment were delivered to Columbia on loan for Wood's use. That was the beginning of the Columbia University Statistical Bureau.[14]

The IBM equipment at Columbia became a valuable asset to the University. It was used by several academic departments as well as by the Statistical Bureau. The Astronomy Department used the equipment to check the computations in hitherto unverified astronomical tables. This led to the establishment of the Watson Astronomical Computing Laboratory at Columbia. The Bureau of Collegiate Educational Research employed the machines for the statistical analysis of test scores. All the while Wood and his assistants in the Statistical Bureau, in collaboration with the engineering and laboratory staffs of the IBM Corporation, experimented with mechanical scoring techniques. Their first success came in 1932 with the modification of an IBM tabulator to score the Strong Vocational Interest Blank.[15]

The Strong interest measure, first published in 1927, was widely recognized as a useful device for student counseling. Its principal disadvantage was the expensiveness of scoring it. The responses of the student had to be compared to the response patterns for 39 different occupational groups. Wood remembers that the cost was nearly $5 per student, even when using the hand-sorted punched card method developed by Phillip J. Rulon of Harvard University. The new scoring procedure was an adaptation of Rulon's method to the full-speed efficiency of an IBM tabulator. It reduced the cost of scoring to about 50 cents per student, thereby permitting a large increase in the use of this helpful device. The total number of scores on this test reported by Wood's office during the year 1932 was 160; during the second half of 1933, with machine scoring in full use, the number increased to 3,105. The Strong Interest Blank was used much more widely thereafter as a counseling device.[16]

The tabulator and punched card technique used for scoring the Strong test did not really solve the scoring problem. It was unsuitable for most objective tests. It was too slow and it was still too expensive. Wood had in mind a machine that would score an inexpensive answer sheet with the speed of electricity. The engineers at IBM, working closely with Wood and his staff at Columbia, had experimented with electronic scoring. Their models employed either a scanning device to read the answers or the analogue principle, in which the score was recorded on an ammeter in units of electricity when the electric circuits in the machine were closed by a graphite pencil mark on the answer sheet. The latter was a very promising idea, except for one frustrating obstacle. The amount of electricity conducted—and thus the score registered by the ammeter needle— varied according to the darkness of the pencil mark. This problem which had stopped the Statistical Laboratory staff and the IBM engineers for two or three years was solved in 1934 by a high school science teacher.

Reynold B. Johnson, a Michigan school teacher, had independently developed an analogue scoring machine which solved the pencil mark problem with an ingenious yet simple device. Into the tiny circuits closed by the pencil marks Johnson inserted high resistor units of 2,000,000 ohms which stepped up the total resistance to the extent that variations in the marks (500 to 5,000 ohms) were no longer significant. An IBM salesman found out about the invention and Johnson was promptly invited to New York. From a description of the machine which Johnson had forwarded to him, Wood saw, to his great pleasure, that the basic problem had been solved. IBM hired the young inventor and developed the first commercial test scoring machine—the IBM model 805 which became available in 1935. Reynold B. Johnson is now head of the IBM Advanced Systems Development Division in Los Gatos, California.

Full credit for the brilliant solution to the technical problems in the test scoring machine belongs to Reynold B. Johnson. Yet had it not been for Wood's early initiative, and for Thomas J. Watson's interest in education, the development of Johnson's machine might have been delayed for years. In the opinion of John Flanagan, "The IBM test scoring machine would never have been developed had it not been for Ben."[17] Certainly the scoring machine itself was never a large money-maker for the IBM Corporation, and the salesmen have always regarded it as an orphan, if not an oddity. It was developed largely as a service to education.[18] It must be hastily added, however, that the principle on which the machine operated revolutionized the technology of mechanical computation and had an enormous commercial value. The test scoring machine is said to have been the first electronic analogue computer. Wood's role in developing the machine was aptly described by Reynold B. Johnson: "It was only one example," he said, "of Wood's ability to visualize the relation between technology and education and to spur people like Thomas J. Watson and Nicholas Murray Butler (then President of Columbia University) to a common, fruitful action. He is a courageous innovator in the field of education."[19]

"The revolutionary character of the influence of the improved scoring machines, not only on the testing movement but on our whole educational philosophy, has never adequately been explained or understood," Wood has written.[20] Unquestionably the development of the scoring machine was a major breakthrough for the testing movement. It permitted an unprecedented expansion of large-scale testing activities and huge reductions in the cost of testing. For the first time test booklets were reusable. One of the first examples of the economies which machine scoring made possible came from Connecticut. The state high school testing program there operated on a very limited budget during the depression years. In November 1936, the Cooperative Test Service gave Connecticut the manuscripts of four tests, but the state testing agency had nearly exhausted its funds after printing barely 5,000 copies of each. Thereupon the State borrowed a scoring machine and bought thousands of answer sheets, which cost very little, and by mid-December had tested 38,000 high school students and planned to test 50,000 by the end of the year. The total cost per pupil for the battery of four tests was not more than eight to 10 cents.[21] The separate, inexpensive answer sheet was an enormous spur to the testing movement. Arthur Traxler said in an address at the 1953 Invitational Conference on Testing Problems, "I like to think that the test scoring machine has been to the testing business what the Model-T Ford was to the automobile industry. If the Model-T put America on wheels, the test scoring machine has put the youth of America on objective-test answer sheets."[22]

The increasing use of machine scored answer sheets in testing programs throughout the United States may not have been an unalloyed blessing. The answer sheet has tended to fix the form of the examination. Some test makers have shown a great deal of inventiveness within the form, but they have not been able to transcend the limits of the machine. No one has been more conscious of this problem than Arthur Traxler of the Educational Records Bureau. "The use of the kind of answer sheet required by the fixed response position and the fixed fields of the scoring machine has tended to force objective testing into a kind of strait jacket—in truth, a somewhat loose fitting and benign strait jacket, but a strait jacket nonetheless," he said in 1953. "The four- or five-choice, discrete test item has become virtually standard so that, except for differences in content, the parts of many of our standard tests are almost as interchangeable as the housing units in a Levittown. The test scoring machine is not, of course, wholly responsible for this development, but I think it has accelerated a trend that might have been present regardless of mechanical means of scoring."[23]

Ben Wood was a consultant for IBM continuously from 1928 until 1956, and is still periodically called upon informally. He participated in a number of educational projects at IBM other than the development of the test scoring machine. Not the least of that corporation's educational problems by the early 1930's was an internal one of educating and training personnel and customers in the use of its increasingly sophisticated computers. Here Ben Wood saw a unique opportunity for American education to assist and and have a healthful influence upon American business. Utilizing his good will and vast power of persuasion, he convinced Thomas J. Watson that correct educational theory and methods were as important to IBM's educational operation as to that of a university.[24] In 1942 Watson brought in a professional educator, Dwayne Orton, President of Stockton College, to develop an educational institution at IBM. "While a consultant, Dr. Wood was associated in many ways in the development of educational work at IBM," wrote Thomas J. Watson, Jr., the present chairman of the board of directors. "Closed-circuit television for classroom use in customer engineering education and research in the construction of Arabic and Chinese typewriters were projects on which he worked, and illustrate Dr. Wood's interest in the relationship of business to education."[25]

*In 1936 Ben Wood and IBM engineer Reynold B. Johnson look at the
IBM model 805, the world's first commercial test scoring machine.*

There were many indications by the late 1930's of a new interest in
developing a modern educational technology. The foundations were
receiving innumerable requests for subsidies to support the construction of new devices to aid teaching and educational research. In
response to the mounting number of such applications, the Carnegie
Foundation created the Committee on Scientific Aids to Learning,
a screening committee that would decide which proposals were
most promising. Wood served on this committee during its five-year
existence (1937-1942), along with James B. Conant, President of
Harvard; Vannevar Bush, Dean and Vice President of Massachusetts

Institute of Technology; Frank B. Jewett, Vice President of the American Telephone and Telegraph Company and President of Bell Telephone Laboratories; Bethuel M. Webster, a New York attorney; and Ross G. Harrison, of Yale University. Among the projects which this committee recommended for foundation support was the development of the matrix multiplier unit devised by L. L. Thurstone and Ledyard R Tucker, which converted the IBM test scoring machine into an instrument for research. This device greatly accelerated the statistical work which Thurstone was then engaged in at Chicago and which led to his primary mental abilities tests.[26]

The number of new technological developments that have occurred during the past decade, and which are applicable to education, indicate to Wood that education has reached the threshold of a new era. The new educational technology that is struggling to be born will doubtlessly produce whole new families of educational machines. "While it is neither possible nor particularly desirable to rank the new discoveries in importance, it is difficult to avoid the use of superlatives in discussing the multiple contributions and dynamic learning forces released by what we have come to call *programed instruction.*" He especially recommends a a recent book by Wilbur Schramm, *Programed Instruction Today and Tomorrow.* "This book indicates clearly the nature and magnitude of the presently realized contributions of programed instruction and of the much greater contributions which will certainly be developed within a few years."[27]

Wood also foresees a major role for electronic information retrieval devices in the individualized education of the future. "In these times of almost daily technological 'miracles,' I can think of nothing more spectacular than the advances in efficient information retrieval devices, and their multiple revolutionary impacts on learning anywhere, at home, or in the schools, where devices already on the market promise (at long last) to break the stranglehold of typical graded classroom tropisms on both teachers and pupils. The most recent and arresting example of an effective information retrieval facility to promote efficient independent learning by the pupil is the carrel invented by the genius of Sol Cornberg [the Cornberg Student-Paced Study Station]."[28] When giant computers were first coming into existence a decade ago, Wood recognized that electronic brains could free men's minds. He inevitably concluded that the application of electronic brains to education would free teachers' minds.

The National Teacher Examinations

EN WOOD'S commitment to educational reform has inevitably involved him in controversy over the training and qualification of teachers. The success of his campaign for individualized instruction depends ultimately on the extent to which classroom teachers believe in the idea and are capable of implementing it. Ultimately it is a question of how the teachers are trained and what kind of people they are. The logical point of attack would be the curriculum and educational philosophy of the teachers colleges and departments of education. Wood chose a different strategy. He has never had much influence in the teachers colleges, not nearly enough to reshape teacher training programs. He decided long ago that his major effort had to be an educational campaign to enlighten classroom teachers and school administrators. This effort has been dealt with elsewhere.

Wood's only immediate demand upon the teacher training institutions was that they approve for certification only intelligent, well educated, and reasonably sensitive and cultured persons. "We must find a way of restricting our choice of new teachers to educated persons," he wrote in 1940. "We must not yield to the temptation of placing on tenure uneducated persons merely because they are personable, likeable, kind and patient with children."[1] In questioning the intellectual qualification of many members of the teaching profession, and Wood was doing just that, he rubbed the teacher training institutions on a sensitive spot.

When Ben Wood turned his attention to the teaching profession in the 1930's, it had already received a great deal of bad publicity because of its low intellectual standards. State and national college testing programs, beginning with the Pennsylvania Study, did much to attract attention to the problem. On the scales of test scores, teacher candidates ranked consistently low. The 273 seniors in Pennsylvania teachers colleges who participated in the examination of 1932 ranked below all the preprofessional school students and even below the business majors. They ranked only slightly higher than the secretarial students. Prospective teachers in liberal arts schools tended to make slightly higher scores, but they also were decidedly mediocre students.

This evidence from Pennsylvania about teacher trainees was supported by the results of four annual testing programs inaugurated in 1931 by George W. Frasier, President of the Colorado State College of Education, Greeley, Colorado. This study was sponsored by the Teachers College Personnel Association and represented the first national testing program undertaken by American institutions of higher learning. In a 1936 report on the study, *Time* magazine quoted Wood as saying: "Students in teacher training schools . . . are substantially lower than comparable liberal arts students in the scores which they secure in nearly all tests . . . of intelligence, mathematics, foreign languages, natural science, [and] social science." He said 60 per cent of the students enrolled in professional education courses were below the average of liberal arts college freshmen. "Many of these students are literate only in the legal sense of the word."[2]

Central to the problem of improving the intellectual caliber of the teaching profession were the notoriously low admission standards in most of the nation's teacher training institutions. An open-door admission policy combined with institutional and financial pressures to keep up enrollment during the depression years led many teachers colleges to grant teaching degrees to almost anyone who walked through the gate and spent four years in classes. Wood noted in 1936 that teachers colleges were admitting almost illiterate students whose "presence in professional educational classes is inexcusable from any viewpoint that is consistent with professional integrity as opposed to institutional loyalty." He advised the teachers colleges to choose between two alternatives if they meant to maintain professional standards. They must either practice selective admission or prepare the less qualified students for other careers. "My point is that if teacher training institutions continue to admit students of nonprofessional caliber, they are morally bound to do at least two things: (1) keep them out of professional education classes, and (2) provide learning facilities which are appropriate to their individual abilities and needs."[3]

Wood quickly dismissed one proposal for upgrading the profession by making teacher training a five-year course. The student who could plod through four years could just as easily plod through five. "My skepticism regarding the influence of such prescriptions in the future is based upon my observations of their influence in the past. Prescribed units, credits, and time-service requirements have failed to maintain professional standards in the past, and they will fail in the future. . . . Let us remove bureaucratic bookkeeping of time served and credits at least from the center of the stage and devote ourselves to an honest and continuing effort to ascertain the professional promise and qualifications of individual candidates regardless of credits, units, or previous conditions of servitude."[4]

One possible and promising solution was to raise the standards of teacher training institutions by a policy of selective admission. This proposal appealed to Ben Wood because he suspected that the difficulty of attracting good students into the teaching profession was bound up closely with the low academic prestige of most teachers colleges. Higher admission standards would improve the reputation of the colleges and thereby attract superior students. In a study in 1941 of teachers colleges which had adopted a selective admission policy, Wood reported: "It seems clear that the teachers colleges which follow the pattern of admission policies and practices with which we are here concerned are notably superior in the functions measured and implied by the English, General Culture, and Contemporary Affairs Tests not only to the other teachers colleges but to the liberal arts and other types of colleges in the program. Teachers colleges can attract and hold, and do attract and hold, the better high school graduates."[5] This conclusion was confirmed in a follow-up study of the same teachers colleges in 1956.[6]

Selective admission was not a practical alternative to the many state colleges which were then required by law to admit any high school graduate from the state regardless of his qualifications. As the teacher surplus of the 1930's became the critical teacher shortage of the postwar years, another and almost insurmountable pressure against greater selectivity arose. Selective admission by only a few colleges would not substantially improve the teaching profession. It would mean a policy, Wood said, of plugging a few keyholes upstairs while leaving the cellar door wide open. Moreover, selective admission by itself might well work an injustice on the students of the selective institutions. After their rigorous course of training they would have to enter the market to compete with "job seekers who are often grossly inferior but whose credentials are often more convincing works of art."[7]

It seemed to Ben Wood more feasible to erect a barrier against incompetent teacher candidates at the end of their training program —at the point of hiring—rather than at the beginning. Although not the ideal way to solve the problem, it seemed to be the only practical way. The situation called for a comprehensive examination administered by the local school board which would hold the candidates for teaching jobs to certain minimum standards of intellectual and professional competence. Such an examination would also provide a means for recognizing the superiority of students trained in more selective colleges. "Unless some such comparable bar is placed at the point of employment, institutions which really desire to raise standards may be indefinitely stymied by the competition of non-selective neighboring institutions that have and exercise the authority to issue legally valid credentials."[8]

A small teacher examination program had existed since 1932, when the school authorities of Providence, Rhode Island, asked the Cooperative Test Service for a special edition of its tests for use as one phase of their teacher selection procedure. Several other cities soon followed the example of Providence. It was a temporary service and it had little prospect of continuing beyond 1940, at which time the Cooperative Test Service's subvention would expire. Making the special forms caused the agency considerable labor and expense. Wood advised the superintendents of the various school systems in 1938 that the teacher examination would ultimately have to be discontinued for financial reasons.

For several years Ben Wood had been trying to persuade the Carnegie Foundation to underwrite a national teacher examination program. The Foundation anticipated a furious reaction from many teachers and teachers colleges and was not eager to get involved. In 1938 Wood finally persuaded Walter A. Jessup, the president of the Carnegie Foundation, to give it a try. The occasion was a chance meeting of the two men on a Paris street corner. The agreement may have been the only method Jessup could think of to free himself from the persistent Wood and complete his tour of the city.

The new teacher examination program got under way in 1939, sponsored by the American Council on Education and financed by a generous grant from the Carnegie Foundation. It operated under the immediate supervision of Ben D. Wood, director, and the National Committee on Teacher Examinations of the American Council on

Education. The task of constructing, administering, and scoring the examinations, and of reporting the results to the school authorities, was assigned to the Cooperative Test Service. It was instructed to make new forms of the examinations each year to keep the tests sensitive to changes in the curriculums of the colleges and to new developments in the subject matter fields.

The first forms of the National Teacher Examinations were put together with the utmost care during the winter of 1939-1940 under the supervision of John C. Flanagan, associate director of the Cooperative Test Service, with the assistance of Frederick B. Davis and Charlotte Croon Davis. The general nature of the examinations was determined by conferences with school officials and by the information gained from questionnaires sent to school superintendents. On the basis of this information, outlines were made of each test unit and these, aggregating 312 pages, were sent to critics in all parts of the country. The revised outlines were then used as guides for constructing 5,500 test items. In December these items were pretested and the results analyzed. After the trial testing, the forms—arranged in 19 separate tests—were again submitted to test critics for a final revision. On March 29-30, 1940, the examinations were administered to 3,726 teacher candidates in 25 test centers from Boston to Des Moines. David G. Ryans directed the administration of the program. In accordance with the wishes of the superintendents, one third of the examinations or four hours of testing time was devoted to contemporary affairs and general culture. The test items on the latter section ranged from current social problems to fine arts and literature. The two-day examinations also included tests of verbal ability and reasoning, a test of professional knowledge, and several subject matter tests.[9]

The National Teacher Examinations caused an enormous furor in educational circles, despite the elaborate precautions taken by the Cooperative Test Service to allay criticism by ensuring examinations of high quality. Critics warned that the examinations would force teachers colleges to concentrate too much on "mere fact-gathering," that they would not test teaching ability, and that they would inculcate unwholesome attitudes toward teaching. Much of this criticism was irrelevant, as Wood pointed out in letters and articles of reply and rebuttal. He reminded the critics that the examinations were intended as only one phase of the teacher selection process; that they tested not only factual knowledge, but the ability to use facts—to think; and that they did test essential elements of teaching ability,

ROLLIE MC KENNA

Good education requires teachers with high intellectual standards.

such as the ability to apply knowledge and to make sound generalizations. As for their effect upon teaching, Wood said, "the committee felt that there was only one choice between the realized dangers of the current system of selection and the potential dangers of a carefully watched experiment in the use of comparable examinations as an addition to the currently used bases for selecting new teachers."[10]

The examinations' most renowned critic was doubtlessly President Albert L. Rowland of the Pennsylvania State Teachers College at Shippensburg. He also raised the most fundamental point of objection in an address denouncing the examinations at the annual meeting of the American Association of Teachers Colleges—the examinations would tend to establish a national and uniform academic standard for all teacher training institutions which President Rowland thought was probably impossible, certainly unnecessary, and absolutely undesirable. Uppermost in his mind was the effect such a standard would have on the smaller and academically weaker institutions.

President Rowland recalled a story, written by Helen Reimensnyder Martin, in which a Pennsylvania country school board preferred a graduate of Millersville Normal School to a graduate of Harvard University. "The incident has amused many readers, as the author intended it to do, but it is more than likely that the school board was right and that the Millersville graduate was actually better prepared to serve in the schools of that community than would have been his more erudite competitor from Cambridge." According to him, the nearly autonomous teachers colleges, operating within a decentralized educational system and meeting the standards imposed by their regional accrediting organization, were mainly responsible for keeping alive the vital, progressive spirit of American education. The nation has made progress toward more effective teaching, he said, "not because the teacher candidates have studied textbooks in preparation for fixed examinations, but because they have lived in the atmosphere of institutions designed to provide over a period of years the associations, contacts, and experiences which will produce such a result. . . . Moreover, it is likely that the proposed imposition of a nationwide examination service powerfully supported by leading school administrators will alter the character of these institutions, reduce their prestige, and ultimately destroy them."[11] The real question was the survival of the Millersville Normal Schools as they then existed. As Wood had written in 1936: "It is an open secret that one of the conflicts involved in this problem is between institutional survival and the maintenance of professional standards."[12]

The National Teacher Examinations have gained greatly in popularity in recent years, although they are still somewhat controversial. The number of candidates tested increased from 13,122 in 1953 to 68,860 in 1963. Perhaps the examinations are only now entering upon a period of wide and effective use. In retrospect it appears that to this date, at least, both the fears and the hopeful expectations aroused by the examinations were somewhat unrealistic. It is most improbable that the examinations in the 25 years of their existence have destroyed any educational institution. If they have contributed to the improvement of a few teachers colleges, the reason has evidently been a voluntary effort on the part of college administrators to improve their institutions.

"Air-Conditioning" America

EN D. WOOD is first and foremost an educational reformer. He probably prefers to be called just an educator. Yet his definition of education is so broad and so laden with social implications that it has inevitably made him an outstanding citizen and patriot. Wood's activities in the Second World War illustrate very well the civic implications of his definition of education. He served through the Second World War, or the second phase of the World War as he aptly describes it, as the civilian chairman of the Joint Advisory Committee on Aviation Education. This committee was established early in 1942 to coordinate the activities of the Civil Aeronautics Administration and the United States Office of Education in adjusting American education and thinking to the new realities of the air age. He was a suitable man for the chairmanship of this committee because of his recognized position among American educators and also because his own mind had made the adjustment years before.

Ben Wood's first close contact with airplanes during the First World War left a deep impression on him. He says that as he watched one particular British plane circle his Army camp in Virginia, he remembered Tennyson's prophetic poem, *Locksley Hall* or perhaps it was the stanzas in Thomas Gray's *Luna Habitabilis.* He recites the latter from memory, as translated from the Latin:

> *"The time will come when thou shall lift thine eyes*
> *To watch a long-drawn battle in the skies,*
> *While aged peasants, too amazed for words,*
> *Stare at the flying fleet of wondrous birds.*
>
> *England, so long the mistress of the seas,*
> *Where wind and waves confer her sovereignty,*
> *Her ancient triumphs yet on high shall bear*
> *And reign the sovereign of the conquered air."*

The poet wrote this prophecy in the year 1737, although it might well have been written on the eve of the Battle of Britain. That, Wood adds, is real future-mindedness. The commercial and military potential of airpower, and its sweeping social and educational implications, was never far from his mind after 1917.[1]

During the interwar period Wood kept himself informed about the advance of the aircraft industry in the United States and paid especial attention to the remarkable aeronautical advances of the German people under Hitler. He saw that not only was Hitler preparing the pilots for a future *Luftwaffe* in the glider clubs that were being organized throughout Germany, but that the Nazis were also taking care to induce a state of national air-mindedness through the educational system. Elementary school students were learning arithmetic by adding and subtracting numbers of airplanes. Until 1934 Wood held a commission in the Military Intelligence Reserve Officers Corps. He decided that the best way to perform his duty was to keep himself informed about airpower and periodically to send reports to his superiors in Washington about the military potential of the airplane. The non-air-minded Army command of that time, the same Army command that had cashiered General Billy Mitchell for his heretical air-age ideas, must have regarded Wood as something of a nuisance. His commission was not renewed in 1934 on the grounds that he had failed to attend summer camp.

A number of civilians in private life and in the government shared Ben Wood's growing alarm about the failure of the American people and the military to adjust their thinking to the air age. They did what they could in their individual capacities. Winthrop Rockefeller, who founded Air Youth of America in 1937, performed invaluable educational work among the young generation. One of his educational methods was to encourage and to coordinate the activities of model plane builders in the United States. Winthrop Rockefeller was later hailed as the "first to realize fully young America's appetite for aviation."[2] Another forward-looking citizen was Assistant Secretary of Commerce for Air Robert H. Hinckley, who also became the director of the Civil Aeronautics Administration when it was established in 1938. He realized that the critical shortage of trained aviators in the United States might be disastrous if this country were drawn into the war that seemed imminent in Europe.

Robert Hinckley's major contribution was the establishment of the Civilian Pilot Training Program under the C.A.A. to train young men in the colleges and universities. He simply bypassed the military.

By the time of the Pearl Harbor attack, more than 700 institutions were involved in the program and had issued certificates to more than 70,000 civilian pilots. Commenting on Hinckley's work, Wood said, in 1942: "Without his far-sighted work we should have less than 30,000 certificated flyers in the country instead of the 100,000 which we now actually have. In addition he has produced more than 2,000 certificated flying instructors and has saved from bankruptcy and dissolution a large number of private flying schools, each of which is now worth its weight in gold."[3] By December 7, 1941, the military had trained only 3,000 flyers. The Army had to be literally blasted into the air age.

Ben Wood established contact with Assistant Secretary Hinckley in March 1941. He had read an article in the *New York Times* which quoted Hinckley as saying that the country needed "air-conditioned, not merely air-minded youth" and that aviation training should logically begin in elementary school rather than in college. "I agree very strongly with both points," Wood wrote in a letter to Hinckley on the following day, "and would like to know what has been done and what is being planned in order to get the elementary schools of the country active in air-conditioning American youth."[4] In November, Wood was summoned to Washington for a conference with Hinckley and a discussion about the problem of air-conditioning education. Before the end of December, 1941, he had a master plan outlined which attacked the problem from several directions.[5]

The main problem, as Wood, Hinckley and others saw it, was not to call attention to advances in aviation, but to reshape American thinking in terms of the air age. Most literate Americans of 1941 were reasonably well informed about the science of air flight. Newspapers and magazines had reported the technical progress of aviation with a fanfare that was monotonous. But to the average American, the developing airplane was merely an interesting curiosity. Air travel to most people was still the daring, barnstorming stunts of the Eddie Rickenbackers. They had not yet fitted the airplane into their everyday thinking and could not at all see its enormous social, economic, geopolitical and strategic implications. A Japanese air attack on Pearl Harbor was almost literally unthinkable, even to men as responsible as Admiral Husband E. Kimmel and General Walter C. Short, who were also caught napping. As Assistant Secretary, Hinckley described the problem: "The main handicap to mass flying, all along, has been that travel in three dimensions is an awesome thing to two-dimensional people. I can remember that solid geometry seemed much more difficult than plane geometry. The air is a strange new element to man. And it will be taken in stride, as a matter of course, only by people who have learned the principles of flying in their youth and have applied those principles in actual practice. After that the fearful mystery is gone. Flight is then a matter of some principles in physics, like a change in the temperature. I call this process the 'air-conditioning' of people. . . . We must have whole generations of people who are air-conditioned."[6]

The program which Wood directed operated on several levels, but it had the single purpose of air-conditioning the American people. Part of the program was aimed at the general public or, as Wood described it, "directly at all intellectual and age levels of our population, from kindergarten to university, from bootblack to professional leader." It was directed at "making aviation as much a part of the conscious thinking and 'attitude' of our people as schools, churches, railroads, penny newspapers, and radio are now."[7] To reach as wide a public as possible from as many avenues as possible, Wood's committee requested and received the cooperation of the communications media, editorial page writers, and even syndicated cartoonists. He says that it is no accident that so many characters in comic strips "enlisted" in the Army or Navy air services during the war. A speakers' bureau was also established to work through Chambers of Commerce and Rotary and Kiwanis Clubs. The committee was always on the watch for civic meetings called to discuss the building or expansion of local airports. Wood and his friends traveled thousands of miles carrying the gospel of air-mindedness. "We woke up America to the air age almost overnight."[8]

The major part of the air-conditioning program was aimed at the youth of the country, and the best way to get to the young people was obviously through the schools. It had been proposed in Washington that a course be introduced in the high schools on the principles of flight as an introductory course for graduates who would go to flight school. Wood took a longer view and insisted that the entire curriculum be air-conditioned. He suggested a program with the dual purpose of initiating the training of future pilots and navigators and of preparing the future generation of public leaders and citizens for life in a three-dimensional world. The committee accepted this larger definition of purpose and got to work immediately.

Several years might have been required during ordinary times to implement a nationwide curriculum reform of the magnitude that Wood had proposed. The Joint Advisory Committee on Aviation

Education set out to accomplish the reform in seven months. It would involve securing the cooperation of and working simultaneously with state education officers, school superintendents and teacher training institutions throughout the country. It meant a crash program in re-educating teachers and in supplying them with textbooks and materials from which to teach. Such a reform could be accomplished only by presenting it as an essential part of the war effort.

A crash program to produce a 24-volume series of air-oriented textbooks was initiated at Columbia University early in 1942. The books were produced by a group of writers under the supervision of N. L. Engelhardt, each author approaching a standard subject matter from an air-age perspective. As *Time* magazine described the series: "The books (called the Air-Age Education Series) add an aeronautical third dimension to mathematics, physics, biology, history, geography, economics, politics, even literature. History lessons now plug a new crop of aero-heroes (from Leonardo da Vinci to the Wright Brothers). Biology lessons describe what happens to a pilot when he blacks out. Social science lessons picture a post-war world of 'aerial freight trains' and decentralized living. Anthologies of the rich, adventurous literature of flying enliven English lessons."[9] The Macmillan Company, which had agreed to publish and to distribute the series at slightly above cost, received the manuscripts in late June and had the first 20 volumes on the market by August 1. It completed in 38 days a publishing job that ordinarily would have required six months. The first edition of the series probably also held the record for the number of factual errors. The series was savagely criticized on that ground. Wood says that provisions had been made for sending each manuscript to an expert to catch the inevitable errors, but that in many cases the experts were also deeply involved in the war effort and at the last minute sent back the manuscripts unread.

Despite its faults the Air-Age Education Series was an enormous success. Macmillan sold out its first printing of 40,000 copies soon after the schools opened in September and rushed through a second printing. The series was especially popular among the students. In Manhattan, students had converged upon the bookstores to buy copies in advance, unwilling to wait for the schools to distribute the volumes as planned. Ben Wood reported that nearly a million volumes had been distributed by August 1943, and he has estimated that half the high schools adopted the series, which probably included over 90 per cent of the high school students of the country. As he wrote to a friend and participant in the air-conditioning campaign: "It has been my privilege, as it has been yours, to have a ringside seat in watching what, as an educator, I can confidently say is the fastest and most pervasive revolution in high school curriculum adjustment that this country has ever witnessed."[10]

By the early summer of 1942, Wood and other members of his committee had contacted the major teachers colleges to secure their cooperation in the air-conditioning program. A large number of them agreed to offer special summer courses to prepare teachers for the new emphasis on aeronautics. Wood suggested that the colleges adopt a new course which Professors Paul Mort, N. L. Engelhardt, George T. Renner, and he had designed for Columbia Teachers College, entitled "Social and Educational Implications of Modern Aviation." By the end of the summer an estimated 10,000 teachers had taken summer courses in aeronautics designed to help them teach the Air-Age Education Series. For teachers who could not attend college that summer, the University of Wisconsin offered a special correspondence course in air-age education.

It was not in Ben Wood's nature to make the chairmanship of the Joint Advisory Committee a desk job. He had too much restless energy for that. While Dr. Engelhardt supervised the preparation of the textbooks, Wood took over the task of recruiting and directing a group of public speakers—"barnstormers," he calls them—who were to sell the air-conditioning program to schools, teachers colleges, and to anyone else who would listen. He looked for men who were leaders in education and persuasive platform speakers. If they were not yet fully aware of the air age, he quickly made them so. The nucleus of the group was composed of Dwayne Orton, then president of Stockton College and now of IBM's educational and editorial staff, President George W. Frasier and Dean William L. Wrinkle of the Colorado State College of Education at Greeley, Dean H. W. Holmes of the Harvard Graduate School of Education, Professor Frank W. Hart of the University of California at Berkeley, George T. Renner, professor of geography at Teachers College, Columbia University, Edgar Fuller, now executive secretary of the Association of State Chief Education Officers, Professor N. L. Engelhardt and Professor Paul Mort, also of Teachers College, Columbia University and Wood.

An experienced and highly successful public speaker, Wood took over a large share of the work. It is evident from the old, yellowed clippings from local newspapers that found their way into his office files in New York that Wood gave captivating performances on his barnstorming tours. He introduced an address in Springfield, Massachusetts, by quoting the following verse:

"When pictures look alive, with movement free —
When ships like fishes swim beneath the sea,
When men outstripping birds shall span the sky,
Then half the world deep drenched in blood shall lie."

Was it written by a contemporary, a Second World War poet? Not at all; it was an inscription from a headstone in the Kirby church cemetery, Essex, England, and at least 500 years old. The moral was that Americans were caught sleeping at Pearl Harbor because they had failed to exercise anything like prophetic vision. They must at least adjust to the air age that was already upon them. That was the task at hand.

On other occasions Wood taught his audiences lessons in air-age geography or global thinking, as it is now called. He had found that the average person's conception of geographical relation was based on the two-dimensional map of Mercator's projection. "Even the military tended to think of the world as a flat Mercator projection in those days," Wood says. If he asked his audiences what would be the approximate flight path of a Japanese attack upon the Panama Canal, they invariably replied that it would come directly across the Pacific Ocean. He would then demonstrate that the shortest global route was the great circle route, which would direct a Japanese attack on the canal from the Northwest over the city of Denver. The realities of the air age, as Wood told an audience in Oklahoma City, "makes the woman who moved from San Diego to Minneapolis to escape the Japanese bombs look incredibly silly. Actually, it is 300 miles closer to Minneapolis from the nearest Jap bombing point." But the woman from San Diego was in very good company. "Many of our scholars still have a steamship attitude, and their conception of world geography is so arranged," he said at Nashville, Tennessee, in October 1942. American education, he concluded, like the great, fixed guns in the British fort at Singapore, "pointed in the wrong direction, out to sea." According to the newspapers, Wood left his audiences excited about the new air-age education program.[11]

In the midst of his barnstorming, in 1944, Wood suffered a heart attack. It put him in bed for a year and slowed the pace of his life thereafter. In 1945 he resigned as director of the Cooperative Test Service and of the National Committee on Teacher Examination of the American Council on Education. Wood also relinquished the chairmanship of the Joint Advisory Committee on Aviation Education.

Although proceeding more slowly than before, Wood remained active as an educator and as a citizen. He maintained his interest in aviation and served as a consultant to the Air Force during the planning phase of the new Air Force Academy. Its curriculum was of special interest to him. In written proposals and in conferences with the Air Force Planning Board, Wood urged that the curriculum be designed to produce not truck drivers of the air, but liberally educated officers who would represent the United States with distinction at their bases throughout the world. He had in mind a course of study similar to the Columbia College Humanities program. Wood also served as a member of a committee of specialists which evaluated the Aptitude for Service System of the United States Military Academy at West Point in 1952. Since 1950 Wood has served on the Faculty Advisory Committee of the American Assembly, which was established by Dwight D. Eisenhower, when he was President of Columbia University. Wood also helped Eisenhower raise the funds necessary to organize the Assembly. The Ford Foundation was another postwar organization for which Wood helped to lay the groundwork. He served as assistant to Francis T. Spaulding, Commissioner of Education in New York, who was a member of the five-man committee organized to formulate plans and policies for the Foundation. The recommendations which Commissioner Spaulding and Wood worked out, and which summarized the opinion of national leaders throughout the country whom Wood had canvassed, were substantially accepted by the committee and later by the trustees of the Foundation.[12]

The Coming Revolution in Education

EN D. WOOD at 70 is as optimistic and as full of reform fervor as he was at 30. He is still as forward looking. When he reflects upon the past it is not through nostalgia, but to add perspective to the present and to gain more leverage on the future. When he recounts the past he will pause now and then to repeat that he is a very fortunate man to have seen so many of his ideas accepted and put into practice. One suspects that Wood's optimism is, in fact, due less to what has happened, to his successes over the years, than to what he thinks is about to happen.

Ben Wood thinks that education in the west, especially in the United States and Great Britain, is on the threshold of a major breakthrough, a revolution that will make every reform of the past seem trivial by comparison. The changes which he foresees will not only remodel the physical appearance of the school, but will have far-reaching social and moral implications. The breakthrough will come with the culmination of several coordinate revolutions, all of which are discernible at the present moment.

In an address at Cleveland, Ohio, one of the 1963 Jennings Scholar Lectures, Wood outlined his vision of the future of education. "We all remember that H. G. Wells said, 'Civilization is a race between education and catastrophe.' With the stockpiles of atomic bombs already available, we can change the word 'catastrophe' to 'total extinction of all life on this planet.' This is more than enough to make us realize that education is the most indispensable, as well as the most inspiring, of all human enterprises. While atomic developments have enormously increased the burden and obligation of education, we can mercifully find new hope in the fact that other technological and psychological advances have put us at the threshold of a greater revolution in education than has ever occurred or even been dreamed of since the dawn of history. This unprecedented and benign revolution in education will be enforced by necessity and made feasible by several recent inventions, discoveries, and rediscoveries. The revolution, which has already actually begun in the most advanced nations and which in self-defense the most advanced nations will necessarily help spread as rapidly as possible to the underdeveloped and new nations in the world, will embrace not only the traditional intellectual divisions of the curriculum but will for the first time in history hopefully include a successful program in the hitherto stubbornly intractable areas of character development and moral understanding, with social responsibility and constructive motivations securely based on emotional maturity."[1] He then described the separate revolutions that are now under way.

First there is the revolution in educational technology. Wood's interest in the new technology has already been noted. The new machines are only a means to an end, and that end is a greater degree of individualized instruction and self-learning. The result of this aspect of the coming revolution will be a transformation of the role of the teacher. As he said: "In view of the increasing shortage of top-flight teachers, it would be difficult to exaggerate the potentials of the revolution in the more efficient utilization of the available supply of teachers and of teaching talent by team teaching, varied uses of TV presentations (both closed and open circuit), as well as by the massive saving of teachers' time, energy, and perspective from the use of programed instruction in various types of learning machines and paper-and-pencil devices."

The successful and efficient utilization of the new technology and of the teacher depends upon certain other advances, which are also now under way. Wood thinks that at long last the movement toward ungraded schools is taking hold. "We should not 'sell short' the long-delayed and still unhappily slow but sure emergence of the ungraded school which not only removes the most stubborn block to individualized education, but also automatically entails the whole train of flexibilities and adaptabilities of teachers, of teaching goals and methods, of curriculum, evaluation and guidance, which with other related improvements and implementations add up to individualized education."

The revolution in educational methods, Wood predicts, must and will be accompanied or soon followed by a revolution in educational research. Single-track research projects, conceived and managed by one director, will give way to large-scale, long-term research programs, capable of dealing with more fundamental and complex educational questions. "Such research programs would be conceived and planned by teams of advisers. . . . The team of directors would constantly seek help and ideas from all levels of the research program staff, including classroom teachers, community service officers, civic leaders, judges, medical doctors, etc., as well as advisory groups of scholars from the usual education-oriented disciplines, sociology, psychology, psychiatry, etc. The time of the one-man research department and the 'penny-budget' type of research project for one or two or three years has passed as surely in education as it has in industry and military weaponry." The allocation of larger sums of money for larger research programs will tend to accelerate all the other revolutions and bring them to their culmination more surely and quickly.

The research program of an educational system should tap the full resources of the community. The Educational Research Council of Greater Cleveland has demonstrated that the improvement of education can be a total community effort. "Personally I do not know of any other curriculum reconstruction effort with such appropriate and comprehensive goals, with such laudable local support from local foundations, local business and civic leaders, from local lay and religious groups, from local educators representing both administrative and classroom teaching groups; nor do I know of any other such effort conducted with more statesmanlike wisdom and foresight." The Cleveland program has been developed by the imaginative genius of George H. Baird, its executive director.

"Continuing our enumeration of the factors that are making feasible and in fact demanding a basic revolution in education, it seems to me that none is more important than the discovery, or rather rediscovery, that the rationality, reasoning powers, intellectual interest, and learning capacities of infants aged 2 to 6 years are very much greater than has been suspected. This revolutionary 'discovery' has been boldly and clearly announced by Professor Jerome S. Bruner of Harvard University in his 1960 book called *The Process of Education,* published by the Harvard University Press, Cambridge, Massachusetts, in the following paragraph on page 32:

'We begin with the hypothesis that any subject can be taught effectively in some intellectually honest form to any child at any

stage of development. It is a bold hypothesis and an essential one in thinking about the nature of a curriculum. No evidence exists to contradict it; considerable evidence is being amassed that supports it.'

These astonishingly large capacities are dramatically revealed when infants have been released from the traumatically restricting limitations of an inappropriate writing instrument (the pencil or pen), and from the even more traumatically confusing and frustrating inadequacies of our Roman alphabet and of the multiple contradictions and pyramided absurdities of our English spelling conventions."

The two instruments which Wood thinks will contribute most to releasing the energies of young learners and permitting their often underestimated powers of concentration to focus on productive intellectual effort are the typewriter and the Pitman Initial Teaching Alphabet.

The experiment which he and Frank N. Freeman conducted convinced Wood that the typewriter had an extraordinary potential as an early learning aid. Writing on the typewriter was faster, less frustrating, and more attractive than pencil writing. He is still convinced. "It is a question of enabling the pupil to make his letters 'look just like the book,' to increase writing speed so that the very slow pencil-writer will not exhaust his interest or forget what he has started to write before he writes the first word of his sentence, and to reduce the frustrations and too often painfulness of manipulating a pencil before the nerves of the hand and fingers are sufficiently myelinated to permit acceptably aesthetic coordination of the movement of the pencil point. . . . The available evidence indicates that the early use of the typewriter will improve the quality of the child's handwriting, as well as the quality and quantity of his handwritten creative writing; but it should not be necessary to add that, once a child has used a typewriter in kindergarten and first grade, he should have throughout the rest of his school career a portable typewriter (or its equivalent) as a standard part of his school equipment, preferably as a built-in part of his Cornberg carrel (or a similar facility), along with the usual assortment of books, pencils, tables, chairs, learning machines, etc."

The principal obstacle to the wide use of the typewriter when Wood and Freeman first explored its potential in 1928 was the expense involved. The cost of a school system's equipping its kindergarten and elementary classrooms with typewriters was considered to be prohibitive, especially during the depression which followed shortly after that experiment. On the heels of the depression came the war, with its preoccupations and metal shortages. Only in the past two or three years has interest in the typewriter as a learning machine revived. A major typewriter manufacturer is presently trying to develop a simplified equivalent of the typewriter, an inexpensive writing machine that will break through the cost barrier. This project is still under wraps and Wood declines to comment further about it. He does say that the cost of equipping classrooms with typewriters should not be a consideration. "Far from increasing costs, the typewriter and other learning machines and audio-visual learning aids will decrease all costs of education, especially the increasingly intolerable costs of pupil failures and their consequent human and moral degradations. We must invest millions of dollars to save billions of dollars plus savings of incalculable human and moral values."

The effective use of writing machines by infant learners depends in turn upon some measure of alphabet and spelling reform. It will do little good to teach a four-year-old to write quickly and painlessly if he does not learn to read and spell until he is seven or eight. The principal obstacle to early reading and spelling is the nonphonemic character of the Roman alphabet and the consequent inconsistencies in English spelling. Words do not always look the way they sound and syllables that sound the same are not necessarily spelled the same. At present, elementary teachers must spend the larger part of two or three school years teaching children to recognize on paper the basic vocabulary that they hear and use nearly every day. If the alphabet were phonemic and the spelling of sounds consistent, a child who knows the alphabet could recognize almost instantly any written word that he has heard and remembered. Reading would come almost automatically. Such is the great advantage of the Pitman Initial Teaching Alphabet.

"Two years of experimental work in England," Wood said in his Cleveland address, "indicate that children using the Pitman Initial Teaching Alphabet learn to read in about half the time required by comparable groups using beginning books in our traditional orthography, that the experimental children like to read and do more reading on their own initiative than control classes, and that the experimental children more than the control children develop the habit of independent, self-propelled and success-motivated study and learning, attacking as a matter of course new words never before seen by them in print, by the strictly analogical reasoning method made possible by the Pitman transitional alphabet. . . . Successful practice in learning by analogical reasoning, as in learning to read through the medium of the Pitman Initial Teaching Alphabet, will almost surely 'carry over' to and be effective in exploiting more fully one of the most promising and dynamic elements of the educational revolution, that is, learning by discovery, which will probably turn out to be the long-sought breakthrough in the old, old problem of learning how to learn!''

Another development that is hastening the breakthrough in education is the new role that many educational thinkers are designing for the classroom teacher. The new design entails a reordering of the priority of the teacher's duties and teaching objectives. The teacher of the future, Wood said, will concentrate less on teaching in the traditional and authoritarian way and more on helping children learn for themselves. He will reorganize the classroom on a much less regimented basis than at present and will cease to regard himself as the repository and dictator of knowledge. This is not to say that the teacher with his classroom assistants will abdicate the responsibility of teaching. Wood does not suggest that the teacher should become merely the custodian of the learning machines. The teacher will still be involved in the learning situation, but in a much different way than before. His principal responsibility will be to help children think things out for themselves, including the moral implications of knowledge, and the ethics of ordinary social and classroom behavior. The teacher's role should be that of a guide who poses the questions that lead his pupils to a deeper understanding of themselves, of life, and of the world around them.

Within the reordering of priorities and objectives of education that Wood foresees, the development of the child's moral understanding and social responsibility will receive the greatest emphasis. He maintains that it is as much the responsibility of the schools as of the churches to make certain that the political, military, and scientific geniuses of the future are not its moral idiots. "I often recall that the late lamented President Butler of Columbia University used to include in nearly every speech he made the statement that the most basic problems of the human race are fundamentally moral problems. If we, as I think we must, accept President Butler's statement as true, then I think we would be justified in saying that the most important single one of the several discoveries leading to and making possible the great educational revolution which we are now beginning to experience is the discovery about 15 years ago by Ralph H. Ojemann of the University of Iowa of the idea of 'causal orientation' in teaching materials, taught by teachers who are causally oriented." The object of Ojemann's approach is to develop a heightened moral sensitivity by helping children discover in the classroom the rational basis for personal morality and social ethics. It is a direct attack upon the problem of character development.

Ojemann's causal orientation approach is also one of the most promising applications in the classroom of the basic principles of the emerging science of psychodynamics. This is a relatively new discipline, a science of human nature based on biology, physiology, and psychiatry. It promises to add a new and long-sought dimension to the school curriculum from nursery and kindergarten through the twelfth grade and beyond. One of the most lucid writers on psychodynamics is Leon J. Saul, M.D., of the University of Pennsylvania Psychiatric Faculty. Saul maintains that the violence and cruelty in man is symptomatic of unhappiness and frustration. Emotionally mature and stable adults are kind, friendly, constructive, and responsible as parents and citizens. By studying the emotional development of individuals and by identifying sources of frustration, he contends, we can deal with violence and cruelty in society as effectively as we have dealt with typhoid fever or smallpox. He is probably the only psychiatrist who has taught an elementary course in psychoanalysis as a part of the liberal arts curriculum in a liberal arts college.

The science of psychodynamics, Wood said, has far-reaching implications for education. Prevention is always more efficient than the cure and in this case education holds an important key to prevention. Educating children properly, with attention to their emotional and moral development, will help produce emotionally mature adults. Teachers well-grounded in the science of psychodynamics will help to produce emotionally mature leaders and citizens for the future. "Among the most important of the discoveries or rediscoveries that make feasible this long-hoped-for improvement in education, I think history will confirm my opinion that the most neglected and the most strategic is the recent development of the science of psychodynamics."

Such were the several revolutions taking place in education and in related fields that Wood described in his Cleveland address in 1963. The address was optimistic throughout, and for sufficient reason. Each of the developments pointed in the direction of individualized, self-directed, and properly motivated learning, the cause to which Wood had devoted forty years of his life. The goal appeared to be closer than at any time before. Ben Wood's old vision of the future was beginning to materialize.

The Cleveland address was also Wood's statement of a new vision. The breakthrough which he foresaw was more than the advent of individualized education. When the several revolutions in education are completed, they will have an impact far beyond the walls of the classroom. He was saying in effect that the new developments will give education the capability of breaking through the ceiling of the present level of human existence to a higher stage of civilization. He was talking about education as a dynamic force in the social and cultural evolution of *homo sapiens*.

The accelerating accumulation of scientific knowledge has placed almost within the grasp of man control over his own biological evolution and over all the inhabitable spaces of the universe. In recent years Ben Wood has given much thought to this prospect. On the title page of his Cleveland address he inserted a quotation from George Wells Beadle, Nobel laureate and onetime president of the American Association for the Advancement of Science, that bears directly upon this point. "Man's evolutionary future . . . is unlimited. But far more important, it lies within his own power to determine its direction . . . an opportunity never before presented to any species on earth. . . . To carry the human species on to a future of biological and cultural freedom, knowledge must be accompanied by collective wisdom and courage of an order not yet demonstrated by any society of man." Yet this breakthrough, this leap forward and outward of *homo sapiens,* depends upon an equally accelerating accumulation of moral knowledge, wisdom, and courage. And that, Wood contends, is a duty of the educational institutions. Without a strong moral sense, man may use his scientific knowledge for evil purposes and in the end destroy himself. He already has that capability.

The wars and barbarism of the present century are ample evidence that a gap exists between the levels of man's scientific and moral wisdom. Or, from the psychodynamic point of view of Leon J. Saul: "The Western man of today lives in the ultramodern world of shrunken space and limitless atomic power. But he lives an emotional life that is still primitive—a veneer over the emotional life of the cave and the jungle. Physically of the Atomic Age, he lives emotionally in the Stone Age." The educational institutions can play a central role, Wood contends, in closing this gap. They have a clear obligation to do so and the revolutions that are now taking place in education will make it technically feasible. The rational, unfrustrated, and socially adaptable children developed by the new education will grow up to be moral, emotionally mature, and cooperative citizens and leaders. "If I could say only one thing as my farewell to education, it would be to repeat what Horace Mann said in his inaugural address as president of Antioch College in 1853. 'The more I see of our civilization and the only remedies for its evils, the more I fear eminence of intellect when separated from virtue.'"

To understand the social turn of Wood's thought it is necessary to see that he has always been a social reformer as well as an educator. In this sense Wood's career is not unique. The more thoughtful of the progressive educators of his generation were fundamentally social reformers. Permitting happy, well-adjusted children to grow up to be mature and emotionally stable adults was the progressive educators' formula for transforming human society and for making the world a healthier and safer place in which to live. Ben Wood subscribes to that formula. In his Cleveland address he restated it and placed it in a more cosmic perspective.

Sir James Pitman and Ben Wood discuss Initial Teaching Alphabet below portrait of Sir Isaac Pitman, inventor of Pitman shorthand.

The Initial Teaching Alphabet

FTER DISCUSSING Ben Wood's contributions to education at some length with this writer, George D. Stoddard paused momentarily and concluded: "Ben Wood is one of our elder statesmen."[1] It was an apt description of the stature which Ben Wood enjoys among the leaders of American education. Yet in another sense the term is misleading. When Wood retired in 1960, he did not withdraw to the Olympian heights of his city home on Morningside Drive to reign as elder statesman. He is still actively involved in the search for ways and means to make education more responsive to individuals. He still maintains a correspondence with educators and researchers from all parts of the world. When an old friend and colleague asked him why he did not retire to the country to enjoy his leisure, Wood replied that there was too much going on in the world for that. The elder statesmen of education, unlike old soldiers, do not fade away.

During the past three years Wood has given a large part of his time and thought to the reading-failure problem and to the promising solution represented by the Pitman Initial Teaching Alphabet. He has taken up this interest with the same gusto, and almost the same vigor, that was characteristic of Ben Wood 30 years ago. It is not, in fact, a new interest, but an old one revived.

Wood has been an amateur linguist since his college days and was conscious of the spelling and alphabet problems and their retarding effect on reading. But the task of reforming a language used by 250 million people seemed utterly out of the question and he suspected that having two alphabets and forms of spelling would create more problems for children than it would solve. Then, in 1961, he read an article in the October issue of *Think* magazine, an internal publication of IBM, about Sir James Pitman's augmented Roman alphabet and its success in selected schools in England. The thought occurred to Wood that the augmented alphabet might be the long-sought solution to the reading problem. He says that the Pitman method appeared to him to be at least too important a discovery for a responsible American educator to put aside uninvestigated.[2] Shortly thereafter, during a vacation trip to Europe, Wood made a side trip to England and spent a week visiting the schools using the Pitman alphabet.

What he saw in England convinced Wood that the solution to the reading problem for the English-speaking peoples lay at their very fingertips. He had watched children teaching themselves to read with a phonemic alphabet. They would pronounce the words in their books, haltingly and with difficulty at first, sometimes requiring four or five attempts at pronunciation until they finally recognized the sound of a familiar word. Then they would say it correctly and beam in sheer delight at their accomplishment. By matching sounds to written syllables, these English children found learning to read a marvelous adventure in discovering how much they knew already. Wood was told that the children had little difficulty transferring to the standard alphabet and spelling after learning to read with the augmented alphabet. Compared with the initial hurdle of learning to read traditional English, the transition was relatively simple.

As he visited from school to school it became apparent to Wood that the augmented Roman alphabet did more than reduce the time required for learning to read. It had a marked effect upon the pupils' attitude toward learning, toward the school, and toward themselves. They found learning an obviously pleasant experience. The ease with which the pupils learned to read also gave them an eagerness for independent study. Most impressive of all was the effectiveness of the new alphabet in repairing the emotional damage caused by the failure to learn to read by the traditional method. Wood's discovery of the therapeutic value of the augmented alphabet was vividly described by John A. Downing, Research Officer of the Reading Research Unit of the University of London Institute of Education, who accompanied Wood on his trip. Downing was supervisor of the ITA experiments in England.

"After correspondence with Dr. Ben Wood I first met him at 10 o'clock in the morning, on Tuesday 27th March 1962, at Harrow-on-the-Hill Station. I took him to see our experimental ITA class at Roxeth Hill School, at Harrow. Then after our visit there we drove up to the Midlands of England and visited a school in Wolverhampton. This was St. Mary's Roman Catholic School. I have a vivid impression of an experience with Dr. Wood that day. It was in the afternoon at about 4 o'clock when school was closing for the day. The Initial Teaching Alphabet was being used, not only in the beginning reading classes there, but also for helping older children who had suffered failure in reading through traditional methods.

"One of these children was a little girl who had truly suffered in this respect. Not only had she failed to learn to read, but this had affected her personality quite seriously. She had become a *silent* child. Previously it was almost impossible to get her to talk to her own teacher, and the Priest of the Parish had found it impossible to instruct her in religious matters because she would not speak to him. On this occasion when this girl had been in the special class experimenting with the new alphabet for about two and a half months, she astonished me by reading to me without any inhibition. I asked her to come to see Dr. Wood, who was with the Headmaster of the school, Mr. Riley, and without any trouble she followed me there. Her reaction to Dr. Wood was even better than it had been to me. She sat on his knee and read him a story from her book.

"Dr. Ben Wood was very impressed by this event, and especially astonished when he learned from the Headmaster and the Priest of the girl's past history."[3]

Wood suspects that learning to read with the traditional alphabet and orthography may also tend to weaken a child's faith in rationality. Human beings have an inborn intolerance for ambiguity. We are driven by the desire to know, and from an early age we begin to develop a faith in rationality. It is part of our human dignity. For a child of six or seven to discover that written language, one of his basic tools, is constructed in an irrational and arbitrary way can have damaging results. The experience may bring into question, perhaps without his fully realizing it, the intellectual integrity of the teachers who tell him that learning to write and to spell is a rational process. It could destroy his faith in his own rationality. At the very least it is a source of frustration.

The Initial Teaching Alphabet, Wood says, will tend to strengthen the habit of rational thinking and the child's faith in rationality. "This transitional alphabet, which is phonemically consistent and almost automatically compatible with our traditional script, not only avoids impairing or destroying the child's rationality and faith in rationality, but preserves and enhances his reasoning powers and faith in reason and *in himself and in his teachers,* and thus makes the child's *first* contact with the school a rational and successful experience. When we see the effects of reading failure in all its tragic ramifications on pupils of all levels of intelligence, it is difficult to overestimate either the short- or long-term values of Sir James Pitman's contribution to the educational revolution."[4]

Ben Wood came home from England fired with a missionary kind of enthusiasm for the Pitman Initial Teaching Alphabet. In the months that followed he worked assiduously to find money for continued research with ITA and to popularize the new alphabet in the United States. He turned first to the Grant Foundation, which contributed $178,500 from May 1962 through February 1965 to acquaint American educators with the ITA experiments in England and to inaugurate similar experimental programs in this country.[5] The assistance from this foundation is only a portion of the American research funds invested in ITA.

The first stir of public interest in ITA in the United States was the result of a visit by Sir James Pitman and John A. Downing, which Ben Wood arranged and planned in the autumn of 1962. The visit included several dinner meetings with prominent American educators and civic leaders, discussion sessions with school administrators and teachers, and lecture tours by both men. Sir James Pitman told audiences from New York to California about the development of ITA by three generations of Pitmans and about the many implications of the new alphabet for education, for mental health, and for international relations. Downing presented the results of the experiments with ITA in British schools.

The contacts made during the visit by Sir James Pitman and John Downing led to the initiation of several experiments with ITA in the United States. The first major experiment was begun at Bethlehem, Pennsylvania, supported by a $148,000 grant from the Ford Foundation. Experiments were also initiated at Cleveland, Ohio; Minneapolis, Minnesota; and Lompoc, California. Not the least important result of the visit were the offers of financial support by American foundations for the experiments under way in England. As John Downing has written: "the progress of our research work here in Britain would have been much slower without the financial help we received from the Foundations to which our work was introduced by Dr. Wood."[6]

Ben Wood said in the summer of 1964, in a voice that was meant to be quoted: "I take great satisfaction in my contribution to spreading Sir James Pitman's ideas."[7] Certainly it has been a major contribution. He was mainly responsible for the introduction of ITA into the United States. Using his influence and prestige, Wood has also helped to secure in three years foundation grants for ITA experiments totaling nearly half a million dollars. This may well turn out to be the most successful undertaking of his career, and the one with the most far-reaching and important consequences. The implications of ITA for education today and for the revolutionary educational system of the future are many and manifest. Beyond that, the Pitman method represents the most promising step toward language reform since Theodore Roosevelt reopened the war on the conventional English spelling more than half a century ago. Of far greater significance, the spread of the Pitman Initial Teaching Alphabet may in the end carry the ancient Roman alphabet to a higher stage of linguistic evolution. All this Ben Wood became involved in as he approached the age of 70.

This chapter completes this biography of Ben D. Wood, but it would be rash, indeed, to suggest that the adventure with ITA is Wood's concluding chapter. The man seems to be indestructible; his spirit unquestionably is. Whatever endeavor his active and vigorous mind takes him to next, one can predict that it will be consistent with the central purpose of his life. In one way or another it will be concerned with the making of a better world by producing individually educated, properly motivated, and emotionally mature human beings.

NOTE: An *Afterword* to this biography, written by Sir James Pitman and printed in the ITA type face, follows on page 89.

afterwurd

Ben Wood

and ſhe
iniſhial teeᴄhiŋ alfabet
bie

Sir James Pitman

"whær ſhær iſ nœ viʒon ſhe peepl periſh"

"yꝏr œld men ſhall dreem dreemſ,
yꝏr yuŋ men ſhall see viʒonſ"

afterwurd

a man's ies need too bee œpen if hee is too see, but abuv aull his miend aulsœ needs too bee wied œpen if hee is too hav viʒon, reeçhiŋ out for whotever mæ bee good as well as nue.

wee in britæn had scærsly started wiʈh i.t.a. befor BEN WOOD becæm awær ov it: a see-er and a seeer, hee apprehended ʈhe significans ov whot wos ʈhus afoot, and packiŋ his bag hee wos ʈhe first ov meny americans too cross ʈhe œʃhean eeger for informæʃhon and for ʈhe facts for judʒment; returnd eksieted, seezd ov ʈhe potenʃhial magnitued ov ʈhis nue iedea, and determind too act.

still too ʈhis dæ a wunder man, whot must hee hav been at ʈhat æj when a suppœsedly mor œpen ie and miend wer, yeer bie yeer, brækiŋ freʃh ground in sœ meny feelds ov creætiv novelty.

it is hard for us nou too credit ʈhat hee cod hav been mor perseptiv, mor penetrativ too ʈhe fundamental issues ov freʃh iedeas, mor inkwisitiv in pursueiŋ ʈhe lojical ekstenʃhons from his nue persepʃhons, and mor devœted too ʈhe importans ov eduecæʃhon as ʈhe hueman gætwæ too ʈhe cumiŋ kiŋdom.

let us hœp ʈhat wee mæ bee riet in suppœsiŋ ʈhat hee has reesently reept in renued zest and happiness a tieʈh ov whot hee has ʈhus contribueted too eduecæʃhon in ʈhe iŋgliʃh-speekiŋ wurld and too ʈhe fuetuer happiness ov sœ meny millions in ʈhat græt commuenity in whiçh lief is bæst upon reeson, freedom and ʈhe noledʒ ov good and eevil.

perhaps ie miet siŋgl out wun particuelar ov ʈhe meny mœst reesent contribueʃhons ov ʈhis man ov teksan statuer and grætness. ie alœn cod never hav weelded ʈhe inflooens or commanded ʈhe resorses nesessary too hav repeeted in america ʈhe reserçh intoo i.t.a. whiçh ie had açheevd in iŋgland. BEN WOOD heer took up ʈhe torçh wiʈh a jenerus and tiemly subsidy from ʈhe W. T. GRANT FOUNDATION. hee arrænjd a number

afterwurd

ov dinner and luncheon partis at which a very larj number ov rhœs mœst inflœenʃhial in american eduecæʃhonal ʇhaut, incluediŋ his frends, JOHN G. BYLER, ADELE W. MORRISON ov ʇhe GRANT FOUNDATION and ALVIN C. EURICH, ʇhen vies president ov ʇhe FORD FUND FOR EDUCATION, wer æbl tœ heer about ʇhees nue iedeas, discuss and ask prœbiŋ kwestions. ʇhe muenifisent grants from ʇhees foundæʃhons mæd possibl ʇhe virtueally simultæneus start in america and britæn ov larj-scæl eksperimental prœgrams.

ʇhe importans ov ʇhis syŋcroniesæʃhon ov enterpries and ov sucsess bie ʇhe tœ græt uesers ov ʇhe iŋgliʃh laŋgwæj, uesiŋ an **iedentical** iniʃhial teechiŋ meedium, leediŋ tœ an iedentical fienal meedium, cannot bee egsajjeræted. ʇhe cumiŋ ov ʇhe fuetuer wurld laŋgwæj wos ʇhus not œnly advanst sum hundred yeers, but ʇhe very real dænjers ov a touer ov bæbel wer aulsœ request, if not eliminæted, bie ʇhis man's tiemly interest, viʒon and acʃhon.

his appreeʃhiæʃhon ov ʇhe enormusly important "secondaris," which flœ from imprœvment in ʇhe commuenicativ abilitis ov individueals, wos immeediætly creætiv. ʇhe interacʃhon ov wun commuenicæʃhon skill upon anuʇher and upon liŋgwistic ability, ʇhe effect upon ʇhe personality ov ʇhe remœval ov commuenicativ frustræʃhons, ʇhe benefit ov eksploitiŋ ʇhe potenʃhiality ov man tœ ues his reesoniŋ and ʇhe benefits ov self-relieant activity and ʇhe jois ov sucsess and self-confidens wer immeediætly nœtist bie him.

fienally, BEN has aulwæs nœn ʇhat lerniŋ wiʇhout morality is simply informæʃhon. aull ov his acʃhons hav ʇhær rœts in his deepfelt beleef in ʇhe dignity ov man and ʇhe permanens ov eʇhical values.

JAMES PITMAN

Notes

Chapter I: An Introduction

1. Interview with Arthur E. Traxler, July 24, 1964.
2. Telephone conversation with Ben D. Wood, August 28, 1964.
3. Interview with George D. Stoddard, July 21, 1964.
4. Telephone conversation with Ben D. Wood, August 7, 1964.
5. Ben D. Wood to the author, February 16, 1965.

Chapter II: An Unorthodox Beginning

1. The biographical information in this paragraph and succeeding paragraphs came from a series of interviews and telephone conversations with Wood.
2. Interview with George D. Stoddard, July 21, 1964.
3. Ben D. Wood to William E. Weld, October 3, 1951; Ben D. Wood's correspondence files, hereafter referred to as Correspondence Files. Also see William E. Weld and Kathryn Sewny, *Herbert E. Hawkes: Dean of Columbia College, 1918-1943* (New York: Columbia University Press, 1958), 80f.
4. *Ibid.*
5. A. A. Méras, Suzanne Roth, and Ben D. Wood, "A Placement Test in French," *Contributions to Education,* 1 (1924), 247-63; Ben D. Wood, "Comparative Study of the Vocabularies of Sixteen French Workbooks," *Modern Language Journal,* 11 (February 1927), 263-89.
6. C. M. Purin to Ben D. Wood, January 20, 1932; Correspondence Files.
7. Ben D. Wood, "Measurement of Law School Work," *Columbia Law Review,* 24 (March 1924), 225.
8. *Ibid.,* 249, 222-23.
9. Harlan F. Stone to Philip J. Wickser, September 13, 1925 (with an explanatory note by Ben D. Wood); copy in Correspondence Files; Interview with Ben D. Wood, September 1, 1964.
10. Ben D. Wood, "New Type Examinations in the College of Physicians and Surgeons," *The Journal of Personnel Research,* 5 (October 1926), 227-34; (November 1926), 277-83.
11. Ben D. Wood and Charles C. Weidemann, *Survey of College Examinations* (New York: Teachers College Bureau of Publications, Columbia University, 1927).

12. Ben D. Wood to Max Farand, April 24, 1925; Commonwealth Fund Research Letterbook, Correspondence Files.

13. Ben D. Wood, *New York Experiments with New-Type Modern Language Tests* (Modern Foreign Language Study Series, Vol. 1) (New York: Macmillan Company, 1927), v.

14. Interviews with Ben D. Wood, August 10, September 1, 1964.

Chapter III: The Pennsylvania Study

1. From remarks by James N. Rule, Deputy Superintendent of Public Instruction, Pennsylvania, in Ben D. Wood, William S. Learned, and James N. Rule, "The Pennsylvania Study of the Relations of Higher and Secondary Education," *Proceedings of the Association of College and Secondary Schools of the Middle States and Maryland,* Atlantic City, November 30 and December 1, 1928, 23-25.

2. William S. Learned to Ben D. Wood, November 3, 1937; Correspondence Files.

3. Ben D. Wood, William S. Learned, and James N. Rule, "The Pennsylvania Study of the Relations of Higher and Secondary Education," 25; William S. Learned and Ben D. Wood, *The Student and His Knowledge* (New York: Carnegie Foundation for the Advancement of Teaching, 1938), 75, 134.

4. *Journal of Higher Education,* 10 (February 1939), 111-13.

5. William S. Learned and Ben D. Wood, *The Student and His Knowledge,* 43.

6. Ben D. Wood to the author, November 20, 1964.

7. Ben D. Wood, "Teacher Selection: Tested Intelligence and Achievement of Teachers-in-Training," *Educational Record,* 17 (July 1936), 374-75; Arthur E. Traxler, ed., *Guidance in Public Secondary Schools: A Report of the Public School Demonstration Project in Educational Guidance* (New York: Educational Records Bureau, 1939), 1.

Chapter IV: The Doctrine of Individualized Education

1. Eugene R. Smith to the author, January 1965.

2. Lawrence A. Cremin, *The Transformation of the School: Progressivism in American Education, 1876-1957* (New York: Alfred A. Knopf, 1961), 240-50.

3. Ben D. Wood to John Dewey, November 22, 1935; Correspondence Files.

4. *Ibid.*

5. John Dewey to Ben D. Wood, November 27, 1935; Correspondence Files.

6. Ben D. Wood, "The Major Strategy of Guidance," *Educational Record,* 15 (October 1934), 424.

7. Ben D. Wood and F. S. Beers, "Knowledge versus Thinking," *Teachers College Record,* 37 (March 1936), 488.

8. Ben D. Wood to Charles Swain Thomas, April 23, 1936; Correspondence Files.

9. Ben D. Wood, "Continuity in Personnel Work," *News Bulletin of the Bureau of Vocational Information,* 4 (March 1926), 17.

10. *Ibid.,* 18.

11. Ben D. Wood to the author, August 28, 1964.

12. Ben D. Wood, "Major Strategy versus Minor Tactics in Educational Testing" *Baltimore Bulletin of Education,* 13 (September 1934), 7.

13. Telephone conversation with Ben D. Wood, August 28, 1964.

14. *Baltimore Bulletin of Education,* 13 (September 1934), 8-9.

15. Interview with Ben D. Wood, August 10, 1964.

16. *Ibid.*

17. Ben D. Wood, "Need for Comparable Measurements in Individualizing Education," *Educational Record,* 20, Supplement (January 1939), 26.

18. Telephone conversation with Ben D. Wood, August 28, 1964.

19. Ben D. Wood to the author, September 22, 1964.

20. *Ibid.*

21. Ben D. Wood, "Major Strategy versus Minor Tactics in Educational Testing," 10-11.

22. *Ibid.,* 14.

23. Interview with Ben D. Wood, August 10, 1964.

24. Ben D. Wood to the author, September 22, 1964.

25. Ben D. Wood, "The Major Strategy of Guidance," 427.

Chapter V: The Educational Records Bureau

1. Interview with Arthur E. Traxler, July 24, 1964; Ben D. Wood to the author, February 11, 1965; Ben D. Wood, "Origin and Work of the

Educational Records Bureau," *School and Society,* 34 (December 1931), 835-37.

2. *Functions, History and Status of the Educational Records Bureau: A Report to Institutional Members* (New York: Educational Records Bureau, 1961), 2f. Interview with Arthur E. Traxler, July 24, 1964.

3. Hart Fessenden to the author, December 3, 1964.

4. Arthur E. Traxler to the author, January 18, 1965.

5. A. D. Henderson to Ben D. Wood, November 8, 1937; Correspondence Files.

6. Ben D. Wood to the author, January 25, 1965.

Chapter VI: The Cooperative Test Service

1. Ben D. Wood, "The Cooperative Test Service," *Educational Record,* 12 (July 1931), 246.

2. Max McConn, "The Cooperative Test Service," *Journal of Higher Education,* 2 (May 1931), 231; "Report of the Executive Committee of the American Council on Education," *Educational Record,* 12 (July 1931), 206-07.

3. Interview with Arthur E. Traxler, July 24, 1964.

4. John C. Flanagan and E. F. Lindquist, *The Cooperative Achievement Tests: A Handbook Describing their Purpose, Content, and Interpretation* (New York: The Cooperative Test Service, 1936), 4. The original staff of the Cooperative Test Service consisted of Ben D. Wood, as director; Mrs. John W. Woodburn, office secretary; and the following full-time assistants: Margaret W. Moore, Ruth McJimsey, Geraldine Spaulding, and John A. Long. John C. Flanagan joined the organization in 1935 as Statistician and was later appointed Associate Director. Other professional staff members associated with the Cooperative Test Service and still working actively in the testing field are Charlotte Croon Davis and Frederick B. Davis, Leone Chesire, Emma Spaney, David G. Ryans, Anna Dragositz, Mary Willis, and Miriam Bryan.

5. *Ibid.,* 13-14. John C. Flanagan, Frederick B. Davis, and David G. Ryans have extensive bibliographies of articles and statistical reports concerning test performance.

6. Interview with Donald J. Shank, July 22, 1964.

7. John C. Flanagan, *The Cooperative Achievement Tests: A Bulletin Reporting the Basic Principles and Procedures Used in the Development of Their System of Scaled Scores* (New York: Cooperative Test Service, 1939).

8. Ben D. Wood, "Ten Years of the Cooperative Test Service," *Educational Record,* 21 (July 1940), 372.

9. Arthur E. Traxler, ed., *Guidance in Public Secondary Schools: A Report of the Public School Demonstration Project in Educational Guidance* (New York: Educational Records Bureau, 1939), xviii.

10. Ben D. Wood, "Ten Years of the Cooperative Test Service." 373.

11. *The Testing Movement,* American Council on Education Studies, Series 1, Vol. 1, No. 1 (Washington, D. C.: American Council on Education, 1937), 22-23.

12. Ben D. Wood, "The Major Strategy of Guidance," *Educational Record,* 15 (October 1934), 426.

13. Nelson A. Jackson to Ben D. Wood, March 22, 1935; F. O. Holt to David Stevens, December 27, 1934; Henry T. Moore to Ben D. Wood, October 14, 1933; Correspondence Files.

14. Donald J. Shank to the author, February 1, 1965.

15. Eugene R. Smith to the author, January 1965.

16. Ben D. Wood and Ralph Haefner, *Measuring and Guiding Individual Growth* (New York: Silver Burdett Company, 1948).

17. E. F. Lindquist, ed., *Educational Measurement* (Washington, D. C.: American Council on Education, 1951), x.

18. William S. Learned to Eugene R. Smith, March 2, 1936; Correspondence Files.

Chapter VII: Education and Technology

1. Ben D. Wood, "Mechanical Education Wanted: A Defense of *Homo Faber*," *The Harvard Teachers Record,* 1 (April 1931), 46-50.

2. A. P. Hollis, *Motion Pictures in Education* (New York: Century Company, 1926).

3. Ben D. Wood and Frank N. Freeman, *Motion Pictures in the Classroom* (Boston: Houghton Mifflin Company, 1929), xvii-xix.

4. *Ibid.,* 223.

5. *Ibid.,* 214-15.

6. John Flory to the author, February 26, 1965.

7. Ben D. Wood and Frank N. Freeman, *An Experimental Study of the Educational Influences of the Typewriter in the Elementary School Classroom* (New York: Macmillan Company, 1932), 1.

8. *Ibid.,* 71.

9. *Ibid.,* 72-73.

10. Quoted in *ibid.,* 93.

11. Quoted in *ibid.,* 95.

12. Quoted in *ibid.,* 101.

13. Quoted in *ibid.,* 101.

14. Interviews with Ben D. Wood, July 17, 30, 1964.

15. Ben D. Wood, "New Method for Scoring the Strong Vocational Test," *School and Society,* 36 (December 3, 1932), 718.

16. Interviews with Ben D. Wood, July 30, August 10, 1964; Memorandum entitled "Strong Vocational Interest Tests Scored for Columbia College by Columbia University Statistical Bureau" in Correspondence Files.

17. Telephone conversation with John C. Flanagan, July 7, 1964.

18. Interview with Dwayne Orton, August 12, 1964.

19. Telephone conversation with Reynold B. Johnson, September 2, 1964.

20. Ben D. Wood to the author, November 20, 1964.

21. Ben D. Wood to Daniel A. Prescott, December 19, 1936; Correspondence Files.

22. Arthur E. Traxler, "The IBM Scoring Machine: An Evaluation," *1953 Invitational Conference on Testing Problems* (Princeton, New Jersey: Educational Testing Service, 1953), 140.

23. *Ibid.,* 140.

24. Interview with Dwayne Orton, August 12, 1964.

25. Thomas J. Watson, Jr. to the author, September 2, 1964.

26. Ben D. Wood to the author, January 25, 1965.

27. Ben D. Wood, "Revolution in Education," Unpublished manuscript of excerpts from an address given on November 16, 1963, in Cleveland, Ohio, as one of the 1963 Jennings Scholar Lectures, p. 6.

28. *Ibid.,* 7.

Chapter VIII: The National Teacher Examinations

1. Ben D. Wood, "Making Use of the Objective Examination as a Phase of Teacher Selection," *Harvard Educational Review,* 10 (May 1940), 281.

2. *Time,* 28 (July 27, 1936), 26; Ben D. Wood, "Teacher Selection:

Tested Intelligence and Achievement of Teachers-in-Training," *Educational Record,* 17 (July 1936), 375.

3. *Educational Record,* 17 (July 1936), 378, 380.

4. *Ibid.,* 380.

5. Ben D. Wood and Ruth A. Pedersen, "Results of Selective Admissions in Teachers Colleges," *Teacher-Education Journal,* 3 (June 1941), 12-22.

6. Ben D. Wood and Robert D. North, "Teacher Colleges Can Select and Hold Superior Students," *Journal of Higher Education,* 27 (November 1956), 419-26.

7. Ben D. Wood and Ruth A. Pedersen, "Results of Selective Admissions in Teachers Colleges," 21.

8. *Ibid.,* 22.

9. Ben D. Wood, "Examinations for Teachers of Business Education," *Proceedings of the 14th Annual Conference,* National Association of Business Teacher-Training Institutions (1941), No. 22, 5-6; John C. Flanagan, "An Analysis of the Results from the First Annual Edition of the National Teacher Examinations," *Journal of Experimental Education,* 9 (March 1941), 237-50; David G. Ryans, "The Professional Examination of Teaching Candidates: A Report on the First Annual Administration of the National Teacher Examinations," *School and Society,* 52 (October 5, 1940), 276.

10. Ben D. Wood, "National Teacher Examinations," *Childhood Education,* 18 (January 1942), 228.

11. Albert Lindsay Rowland, "The Proposed Teacher-Examination Service," *Harvard Educational Review,* 10 (May 1940), 287, 285.

12. Ben D. Wood, "Teacher Selection: Tested Intelligence and Achievement of Teachers-in-Training," 377.

Chapter IX: "Air-Conditioning" America

1. Interview with Ben D. Wood, August 10, 1964.

2. New York *Daily Mirror,* January 26, 1942; also see Lyle W. Ashby, "Education for the Air Age," *Journal of the National Education Association,* 32 (March 1943), 73-76.

3. Ben D. Wood to George W. Frasier, March 21, 1942; Correspondence Files.

4. Ben D. Wood to Robert H. Hinckley, March 31, 1941; Correspondence Files.

58150

5. Interview with Ben D. Wood, August 10, 1964.

6. Quoted in Lyle W. Ashby, "Education for the Air Age," 74.

7. Ben D. Wood, "Air-Conditioning America and the Schools," *Higher Education and the War* (Washington, D. C.: The American Council on Education, 1942), 129; see also article by the same title in *School Executive,* 61 (March 1942), 27.

8. Telephone conversation with Ben D. Wood, August 7, 1964.

9. *Time,* 40 (October 12, 1952), 74.

10. Ben D. Wood to Gill Robb Wilson, August 17, 1943; Correspondence Files.

11. The above information has been taken from assorted newspaper clippings in Wood's correspondence files.

12. Ben D. Wood to the author, January 25, 1965.

Chapter X: The Coming Revolution in Education

1. The quoted material in this chapter has been taken from an unpublished manuscript of excerpts from the address given at Cleveland.

Chapter XI: The Initial Teaching Alphabet

1. Interview with George B. Stoddard, July 21, 1964.

2. Interview with Ben D. Wood, July 30, 1964.

3. John A. Downing to the author, September 18, 1964.

4. Ben D. Wood, "Revolution in Education," unpublished manuscript of excerpts from an address given on November 16, 1963, in Cleveland, Ohio, as one of the 1963 Jennings Scholar Lectures, p. 5.

5. Ben D. Wood to the author, February 16, 1965.

6. John A. Downing to the author, September 18, 1964.

7. Interview with Ben D. Wood, July 30, 1964.

Bibliography of Ben D. Wood

Books

Measurement in Higher Education. Yonkers-on-Hudson: World Book Company, 1923.

New York Experiments with New-Type Modern Foreign Language Tests. New York: Macmillan Company, 1927.

(With Frank N. Freeman) *Motion Pictures in the Classroom: An Experiment to Measure the Value of Motion Pictures as Supplementary Aids in Regular Classroom Instruction*. Boston: Houghton Mifflin Company, 1929.

(With Frank N. Freeman) *An Experimental Study of the Educational Influences of the Typewriter in the Elementary School Classroom*. New York: Macmillan Company, 1932.

(With William S. Learned) *The Student and His Knowledge*. New York: Carnegie Foundation for the Advancement of Teaching, 1938.

(With Leonard O. Packard and Bruce Overton) *Our Air-Age World: A Textbook in Global Geography*. New York: Macmillan Company, 1945.

(With Ralph Haefner) *Measuring and Guiding Individual Growth*. New York: Silver Burdett Company, 1948.

(With Leonard O. Packard and Bruce Overton) *Geography of the World*. New York: Macmillan Company, 1948. Revised 1953, 1959.

Articles, Pamphlets, Conference Reports

(With J. Carleton Bell) "Solution of Problems in Geometry," *Journal of Educational Psychology*, 11 (September 1920), 316-26.,

"The Measurement of College Work," Report of an Experiment Conducted by the Staff of Instructors in Contemporary Civilization in Columbia College with the Assistance of Professor E. L. Thorndike of Teachers College, *Educational Administration and Supervision*, 7 (September 1921), 301-34.

The Reliability and Difficulty of the College Entrance Examination Board Examinations in Algebra and Geometry. New York: Published by the Board, 1921.

"The Reliability of Prediction of Proportions on the Basis of Random Sampling," *Journal of Educational Research*, 4 (December 1921), 390-95.

"Cooperation in Personnel Work," *Educational Record*, 5 (October 1924), 268-72.

(With A. A. Méras and S. Roth) "A Placement Test in French," *Contributions to Education*. Yonkers-on-Hudson: World Book Company, 1924. V. 1, 247-63.

"The 'New Type' Law Examination: A Reply to Professor Wigmore," *Illinois Law Review,* 19 (February 1925), 442.

"Measurement of Law School Work," *Columbia Law Review,* 24 (March 1924), 225-65; 25 (March 1925), 316-31; 27 (November 1927), 784-826.

"The College Curriculum and Vocational Guidance," *School and Society,* 21 (April 25, 1925), 508-12.

"Measurement in Education," *Proceedings of Intercollegiate Parley, Wesleyan University,* December 1925, 5-10.

"Continuity in Personnel Work," *News Bulletin of the Bureau of Vocational Information,* 4 (March 1926), 17-18.

"Studies of Achievement Tests," *Journal of Educational Psychology,* 17 (January 1926), 1-22; 17 (February 1926), 125-39; 17 (April 1926), 263-69.

"New Type Examinations in the College of Physicians and Surgeons of Columbia University," *The Journal of Personnel Research,* 5 (October 1926), 227-34; 5 (November 1926), 277-83.

(With Charles C. Weidemann) *Survey of College Examinations.* New York: Teachers College Bureau of Publications, Columbia University, 1926.

"A Comparative Study of the Vocabularies of Sixteen French Textbooks," *Modern Language Journal,* 11 (February 1927), 263-89.

"Questionnaire Study of 5,000 Students of French in New York State High Schools," *Modern Language Journal,* 12 (October 1927), 1-18.

"Personal Record Cards for Schools and Colleges," *Educational Record,* 9, Supplement 8 (July 1928), 14-52.

Cumulative Record Card for High Schools. Washington, D. C.: American Council on Education, 1928.

Cumulative Record Card for Colleges. Washington, D. C.: American Council on Education, 1928.

(With William S. Learned and James N. Rule) "The Pennsylvania Study of the Relations of Higher and Secondary Education," *Proceedings of the Association of College and Secondary Schools of the Middle States and Maryland,* Atlantic City, November 30 and December 1, 1928, 23-37.

"What Is the Potential Value of the Teaching Film?" *Nation's Schools,* 3 (March 1929), 1-7.

(With William S. Learned) *Study of Relations of Secondary and Higher Education in Pennsylvania.* Progress Report I, May 15, 1929. New York: Carnegie Foundation for the Advancement of Teaching, 1929.

"Trends of Individual Development," *Proceedings of the Ohio State Education Conference, 10th Annual Session, Ohio State University Bulletin,* 35 (September 15, 1930), 191-94.

"Watch the Individual Grow," *Proceedings of the Ohio State Education Conference, 10th Annual Session, Ohio State University Bulletin,* 35 (September 15, 1930), 252-59.

"The Structure and Content of the Comprehensive Examination for College Sophomores," *Recent Trends in American College Education, Proceedings of the Institute for Administrative Officers of Higher Institutions,* 1931. Vol. 3, 190-207.

"Mechanical Education Wanted: A Defense of *Homo Faber,*" *The Harvard Teachers Record,* 1 (April 1931), 46-50.

"The Cooperative Test Service," *Educational Record,* 12 (July 1931), 244-52.

"The Origin and Work of the Educational Records Bureau," *School and Society,* 34 (December 19, 1931), 835-37.

"The Results of a Testing Program," *North Central Association Quarterly,* 6 (March 1932), 359-70.

"Does the Typewriter Stimulate Learning in the Elementary Schools?" *School Management,* 1 (September 1932), 8-10.

"A New Method for Scoring the Strong Interest Test," *School and Society,* 36 (December 3, 1932), 718.

"The Typewriter in the Grades," *The Grade Teacher,* 50 (January 1933), 350-51, 392.

Basic Considerations in Educational Testing. Presented at meeting of National Education Association in Minneapolis, February 28, 1933. Published by Committee on Educational Testing, May 1933.

"Coordinated Examining and Testing Programs," *Educational Record,* 15 (January 1934), 48-55.

"The Ultimate Basis for Satisfactory College-High School Relations," *Bulletin of the American Association of Collegiate Registrars,* 9 (July 1934), 271-78.

"The 1933-34 College Physics Testing Program," *The American Physics Teacher,* 2, Supplement (September 1934), 129-48.

"Major Strategy Versus Minor Tactics in Educational Testing," *Baltimore Bulletin of Education,* 13 (September 1934), 3-16.

"The Major Strategy of Guidance," *Educational Record,* 15 (October 1934), 419-44.

"Contribution of the Cooperative Test Service to the Use of Tests in the

Counseling and Guidance of Students," *Report of the 13th Annual Meeting of the American College Personnel Association,* held in St. Louis, February 19-22, 1936, 27-30.

(With F. S. Beers) "Knowledge versus Thinking," *Teachers College Record,* 37 (March 1936), 487-99.

"Criteria of Individualized Education," *Occupations,* 14 (May 1936), Section 1, 781-86.

"Teacher Selection: Tested Intelligence and Achievement of Teachers-in-Training," *Educational Record,* 17 (July 1936), 374-87.

"What Adjustment Means to the Educator," *Journal of Adult Education,* 8 (October 1936), 470-72.

Bulletin of Information on the International Test Scoring Machine. New York: Cooperative Test Service, 1936.

"Program of the Cooperative Test Service," *Proceedings of the Institute of Administrative Officers of Higher Institutions,* 1936. V. 8, 109-127.

"Test Scoring by Machine," *Nation's Schools,* 20 (August 1937), 34-36.

"The Work of the Cooperative Test Service," *Conference on Examinations, III,* Dinard, France, September 1938. New York: Teachers College Bureau of Publications, Columbia University, 1939, 291-99.

"The Need for Comparable Measurements in Individualizing Education," *Educational Record,* 20, Supplement 12 (January 1939), 14-31.

An Announcement of a Teacher Examination Service. New York: National Committee on Teacher Examinations of the American Council on Education, 1939.

"Some Fundamental Assumptions in the Production and Use of Comparable Achievement Tests in Academic Subjects at the High School and Junior College Levels," *Research on the Foundations of American Education, Official Report,* 1939. (American Educational Research Association), 142-44.

"Making Use of the Objective Examination as a Phase of Teacher Selection," *Harvard Educational Review,* 10 (May 1940), 277-82.

"Ten Years of the Cooperative Test Service," *Educational Record,* 21 (July 1940), 369-80.

Report of the First Annual Administration of the National Teacher Examinations and Announcement of the 1941 Examinations. New York: National Committee on Teacher Examinations of the American Council on Education, 1940.

"Examinations for Teachers of Business Education," *Proceedings of the 14th Annual Conference,* National Association of Business Teacher-

Training Institutions, 1941. No. 22, 3-10.

(With Ruth A. Pedersen). "The Results of Selective Admission in Teachers Colleges," *Teacher-Education Journal,* 3 (June 1941), 12-22.

"Measuring the Cultural Growth of In-Service Teachers," *New York State Education,* 29 (October 1941), 15-17.

"Scores on National Committee Teacher Examinations, 1940 and 1941," *School and Society,* 54 (December 27, 1941), 625-27.

"National Teacher Examinations: A Reply to Dr. Anderson," *Childhood Education,* 18 (January 1942), 227-30.

"Air-Conditioning America and the Schools." *Higher Education and the War.* Report of the National Conference of College and University Presidents, Baltimore, Maryland, January 3-4, 1942. Washington, D. C.: American Council on Education, 129-33.

"In Memoriam—Herbert Edwin Hawkes, 1872-1943," *Educational Record,* 24 (July 1943), 306-14.

(With Arthur E. Traxler and Warren N. Nissley) "College Accounting Testing Program," *Accounting Review,* 23 (January 1948), 63-83.

(With others) *Survey of Aptitude for Service Rating System at the United States Military Academy, West Point, New York.* No imprint, 1953.

(With Robert D. North) "Teachers Colleges Can Select and Hold Superior Students," *Journal of Higher Education,* 27 (November 1956), 419-26; 465.

"Testing—Then and Now," *1956 Invitational Conference On Testing Problems,* November 3, 1956. Princeton, New Jersey, Educational Testing Service, 1957, 58-66.

"Revolution in Education," *The 1963 Jennings Scholar Lectures.* The Educational Research Council of Greater Cleveland, 1964, 51-72.

Published Tests, 1922-1930

Institute of Educational Research Ancient History Test. New York: Institute of Educational Research, Teachers College, Columbia University, 1922.

Columbia College Placement Examination in German. New York: Columbia University, 1923. With Frederick Betz, G. A. Betz, H. G. Wendt.

Placement Test in French. Yonkers-on-Hudson: World Book Company, 1923. With Albert A. Méras and Suzanne Roth.

Junior American History Test, Forms A and B. Yonkers-on-Hudson: World Book Company, 1929. With Harry J. Carman and Thomas N. Barrows.

Columbia Research Bureau Achievement Test Series: Forms A and B of twelve standardized high school and college tests with manuals of directions (1924-1930). World Book Company, Yonkers-on-Hudson. Arthur S. Otis, Test Editor:

English: with Harrison R. Steeves and Allan Abbott, 1925-26
French: with Albert A. Méras and Suzanne Roth, 1926-27
Aural French: with Louise C. Seibert, 1930
Italian (Experimental Edition): with Howard R. Marraro, 1928
German: with C. M. Purin, 1926-27
Spanish: with Frank Callcott, 1926-27
Algebra: with Arthur S. Otis, 1927-30
Algebra: with Jacob S. Orleans and Joseph B. Orleans, 1929
Plane Geometry: with Herbert E. Hawkes, 1924-26
Chemistry: with Eric R. Jette and Samuel R. Powers, 1927-29
Physics: with Hermon W. Farwell, 1926
American History: with Harry J. Carman and Thomas N. Barrows, 1926

American Council Test Series: Forms A and B of eight standardized high school and college tests with manuals of directions. World Book Company, Yonkers-on-Hudson, 1926-30. Arthur S. Otis, Test Editor:

Beta French: with Jacob Greenberg, 1926-27
Beta Spanish: with Frank Callcott and Robert H. Williams, 1926-27
Solid Geometry: with Henry W. Raudenbush and L. Parker Siceloff, 1928-29
Trigonometry: with Joseph B. Orleans, Henry W. Raudenbush, and L. Parker Siceloff, 1928-30
Civics and Government: with Robert D. Leigh, Joseph D. McGoldrick, and Peter H. Odegard, 1929
Economics: with Horace Taylor and Thomas N. Barrows, 1928-29
Ancient History (Preliminary Form): with Irving W. Raymond and Harold Timmerman, 1928
European History: with Harry J. Carman and Walter C. Langsam, 1928-29

WESTMAR COLLEGE LIBRARY

D45P20-206505